bush theatre

The Bush Theatre presents
the world premiere of

The Kitchen Sink

by Tom Wells

16 November – 17 December 2011

The Kitchen Sink

by Tom Wells

Cast

Kath	**Lisa Palfrey**
Billy	**Ryan Sampson**
Sophie	**Leah Brotherhead**
Pete	**Andy Rush**
Martin	**Steffan Rhodri**

Director	**Tamara Harvey**
Designer	**Ben Stones**
Lighting Designer	**Oliver Fenwick**
Sound Designer	**Matt McKenzie**
Assistant Director	**Olly Hawes**
Dialect Coaches	**William Conacher, Daniele Lydon**
Company Stage Manager (on the book)	**Mary Hely**
Assistant Stage Manager	**Amy Jewell**
Assistant Stage Manager (placement)	**Sarah Barnes**
Costume Supervisor	**Sarah Grange**
Production Sound	**Tom Meehan**
Set Builder	**James Turner-Inman**
Scenic Artist	**Bethany Ann McDonald**

The Bush would like to give particular thanks to UBS and West 12; and would like to thank Rob Hastie, Lucy Oliver-Harrison, Allegra Marland, Laura Wade, Ben Eedle, Trevor at SEEVS, Geoffrey Newton, Jools Moxey at Honeyrose, Philip Sheppard, Judith and Ian Jewell, Paul Roughton at Stage Electrics, Pimlico Plumbers.

Leah Brotherhead Sophie

Theatre includes: *Sum Zero* (Lyric Hammersmith Studio); *Product Placement* (Watford Palace); *Time Warner Ignite 2 & 4* (Waterloo East); The 24 Hour Plays: Old Vic New Voices (Old Vic); *The House of Bernarda Alba* (Tristan Bates); *Eye/Balls, Victory Street* (Soho).

Film includes: *Jess//Jim*.

Radio includes: *The Archers, I, Claudius, The Big Sleep, Danton's Death, The Far Pavilions* (Radio 4).

Leah was the BBC Carleton Hobbs Award Winner of 2010.

Lisa Palfrey Kath

Theatre includes: *Red Bud, Ingredient X, Under the Blue Sky* (Royal Court); *Small Change, Ghosts* (Sherman, Cardiff); *Blink* (tour and Off-Broadway); *Gathered Dust and Dead Skin* (Live Theatre, Newcastle); *Festen* (West End and Almeida); *The Iceman Cometh* (Almeida); *Cardiff East, Under Milk Wood* (National Theatre); *Yerma, Story of an African Farm* (National Theatre Studio).

Film includes: *360, Hunky Dory, Guest House Paradise, House of America, The Deadness of Dad, Maybe Baby, The Englishman Who Went Up a Hill and Came Down a Mountain*.

Television includes: *Pen Talar, Blodau, Poboly Cwm, Inspector Lynley, The Bill, Outside the Rule, Casualty, Green Eyed Monster, Split Second, Magistrates, Mind Games, Lord of Misrule, Soldier Soldier*.

Steffan Rhodri Martin

Theatre includes: *Clybourne Park* (Royal Court); *Mary Stuart, Great Expectations, The Birthday Party, The Crucible, Betrayal, Dealer's Choice, Bedroom Farce, King Lear, Twelfth Night* (Clwyd Theatr Cymru); *The Father* (Chichester); *Richard II* (Ludlow); *Abigail's Party* (Hampstead/West End); *The Tempest, Two Noble Kinsmen* (Shakespeare's Globe).

Film includes: *Harry Potter and the Deathly Hallows, Submarine, Ironclad, The Big I Am, Ali G In Da House, Solomon & Gaenor, Twin Town, Yn Gymysg Oll I Gyd*.

Television includes: *Gavin and Stacey, Con Passionate, Belonging, Heartbeat, Wire in the Blood, Tales from Pleasure Beach, A Mind to Kill, On Queen Victoria's Shoulder, Pobol Y Cwm, Dihirod Dyfed, A'R Dyddiadur Du*.

Andy Rush Pete

Theatre includes: *Sense* (Hen & Chickens); *Anna Karenina* (Arcola).

Television includes: *Casualty*.

Andy trained at the Birmingham School of Acting.

Ryan Sampson Billy

Theatre for the Bush includes: *Sixty-Six Books*, *Monsieur Ibrahim and the Flowers of the Qur'an*.

Theatre includes: *Brighton Beach Memoirs* (Watford Palace); *Canary* (Liverpool Everyman/Hampstead); *Dido, Queen of Cathage*, *DNA and The Miracle* (National Theatre); *A Brief History of Helen of Troy* (Soho/UK tour); *Over Gardens Out* (Southwark Playhouse); *Richard III, Edward II* (Sheffield Crucible).

Television includes: *Fresh Meat*, *After You've Gone*, *Doctor Who*, *Holby City*, *In Denial of Murder*, *Heartbeat*, *Wire in the Blood II*.

Ryan was nominated for TMA Best Supporting Performance in a Play for his role in *Brighton Beach Memoirs*.

Tamara Harvey Director

Tamara is Associate Director at the Bush and was one of the directors for *Sixty-Six Books*, the opening production of the new Bush Theatre. Other plays for the Bush include: *Where's my Seat?*, *Resilience* (as part of Steve Waters' *The Contingency Plan*); *Whipping It Up* in the West End (Olivier Award nominee, Best New Comedy, from the original production at the Bush by Terry Johnson) and *tHe dYsFUnCKshOnalZ!*

In the West End, Tamara has directed *Plague Over England* (also the original production at the Finborough); *One Flew Over the Cuckoo's Nest* (Co-Director) and *Bash* (Trafalgar Studios). Her other theatre work includes *Smash* (Menier Chocolate Factory); *Tell Me On a Sunday* (UK tour); *Dancing at Lughnasa* (Birmingham Rep); *Much Ado About Nothing* (Shakespeare's Globe); *Bedroom Farce* (West Yorkshire Playhouse); *Romeo and Juliet* (Theatre of Memory at Middle Temple Hall); *Timing*, *Who's The Daddy?* (King's Head); *Rock* (UK tour); *Touch Wood* (Stephen Joseph, Scarborough); *Closer* (Theatre Royal, Northampton); *One Flew Over The Cuckoo's Nest* (UK tour); *An Hour and a Half Late* (Theatre Royal, Bath/UK tour); *The Importance Of Being Earnest* (Shakespeare Theatre of New Jersey, USA); *Sitting Pretty* (Watford Palace); *The Graduate* (UK tour); *Young Emma and Something Cloudy, Something Clear* (Finborough); *The Lion, the Witch and the Wardrobe* (Maitisong, Botswana). Tamara spent much of 2010 directing the theatre plays that form an integral part of Roland Emmerich's new film, *Anonymous*. She is a trustee of the Peggy Ramsay Foundation, a selector for the National Student Drama Festival and was a member of the 2011 panel for the George Devine Award for most Promising Playwright.

Olly Hawes Assistant Director

Olly is a Creative Associate at the Bush Theatre.

Directing credits include: *Uncool Religion* (part of Sixty-Six Books at the Bush); *Four Walls* (workshop, Network Solutions); *I'm Charlie* (Associate Director; Cathartic Medicine); *The Circle Game* (Waterloo East and Latitude; OVNV/Network Solutions/David Luff Productions; winner of Time Warner Ignite 3); *blood, fish and bone* (as part of Old Vic New Voices' Arden Project; 3LD, US; and Warner Bros. Theatre, UK); *My County Council* (Nabakov present : tense, Roundhouse); *Skipping Games and Mercury/Battus* (Write by Numbers, Brixton Market); *Trace: Behaviour*, *Absent*, *Dial-a-Nativity* (Bus 18).

Credits as an assistant director include: *Mayfair* (Pentabus, Latitude); *Stuart: A Life Backwards* (workshop, Royal and Derngate); *The Hairy Ape* (workshop, The Southwark Playhouse).

Olly was a finalist for the 2010 JMK Award.

Oliver Fenwick Lighting Designer

Theatre includes: *Julius Caesar, The Drunks, The Grain Store* (RSC); *The Contingency Plan* (Bush); *Mary Stewart* (Hipp theatre, Sweden); *Hedda Gabler* (Gate, Dublin); *Happy Now?* (Cottesloe, National Theatre); *Endgame* (Everyman, Liverpool); *Far from the Madding Crowd* (ETT tour); *The Lady from the Sea, She Stoops to Conquer* (Birmingham Rep); *The Elephant Man* (Sheffield Lyceum /tour); *Kean* (Apollo, West End); *Private Lives, The Giant, Glass Eels, Comfort Me With Apples* (Hampstead); *Jack and the Beanstalk* (Barbican); *Pure Gold* (Soho); *Henry V, Mirandolina, A Conversation* (Royal Exchange, Manchester); *Terms of Endearment* (tour); *Restoration* (Bristol Old Vic and tour for Headlong); *My Fair Lady* (Cameron Mackintosh/National Theatre tour production); *The Caretaker* (Tricycle); *The Comedy of Errors, Bird Calls, Iphigenia* (Sheffield Crucible); *The Doll's House* (West Yorkshire Playhouse); *Sunshine on Leith* (Dundee Rep/tour); *Heartbreak House* (Watford Palace); *A Model Girl* (Greenwich); *The Solid Gold Cadillac* (Garrick, West End); *The Secret Rapture* (Lyric, Shaftesbury Avenue); *Noises Off, All My Sons, Dr Faustus* (Liverpool Playhouse); *On the Piste* (Birmingham Rep); *The Chairs* (Gate); *Follies, Insignificance, Breaking the Code* (Theatre Royal, Northampton); *Tartuffe, The Gentleman from Olmedo, The Venetian Twins, Hobson's Choice, Dancing at Lughnasa, Love in a Maze* (Watermill); *Fields of Gold, Villette* (Stephen Joseph, Scarborough); *Cinderella* (Bristol Old Vic); *Hysteria, Children of a Lesser God* (Salisbury Playhouse).

Opera includes: *Samson et Delilah, Lohengrin* (Royal Opera House); *The Trojan Trilogy, The Nose* (Linbury ROH); *The Gentle Giant* (The Clore ROH); *The Threepenny Opera* (for the Opera Group); *L'Opera Seria* (Batignano Festival).

Matt McKenzie Sound Designer

Born in New Zealand, he worked at the Lyric Theatre Hammersmith before joining Autograph in 1984.

He was Sound Supervisor for The Peter Hall Seasons (Old Vic; Piccadilly).

Credits include: *Putting It Together, The Gondoliers, How to Succeed in Business Without Really Trying, Carousel, Babes in Arms, Funny Girl, Music Man, Oklahoma, She Loves Me, Singing in the Rain* (Chichester); *Oh! What A Lovely War, Sweeney Todd, Company, Into the Woods, Merrily We Roll Along* (Derby); *Blues in the Night, Forbidden Broadway, Love Story* (West End); *The House of Bernarda Alba, Journey's End, Tango Argentino, Misery, Long Day's Journey into Night, Macbeth, Sexual Perversity in Chicago, A Life in the Theatre, Swimming With Sharks, Nicholas Nickleby, Lysistrata, The Master Builder, A Streetcar Named Desire, Amadeus, Three Days of Rain, Butley* (West End); *Family Reunion, Henry V, The Duchess of Malfi, Hamlet, The Lieutenant of Inishmore, Julius Caesar, A Midsummer Night's Dream* (RSC); *Flamingos, Damages, After the End, tHe dYsFUnCKshOnalZ!* (Bush).

Ben Stones Designer

Ben trained in stage design at Central Saint Martin's College of Art and Design and went on to win a Linbury Prize commission to design *Paradise Lost* for Rupert Goold.

Theatre includes: *Kiss of the Spider Woman* (Donmar Warehouse); *Creditors* (Donmar Warehouse/Harvey Theatre BAM New York); *Lower Ninth* (Donmar Trafalgar season); *An Enemy of the People*, *My Dad's a Birdman* (Sheffield Crucible); *Beautiful Thing* (Sound, Leicester Square); *Paradise Lost* (Headlong); *The Arab Israeli Cookbook* (Tricycle); *The Mighty Boosh*, *Mitchell and Webb Live!* (Phil McIntyre national tour); *When Five Years Pass*, *The Painter* (Arcola); *Speaking in Tongues* (Duke of Yorks); *Crocodile* (Frank McGuinness premiere for Sky Arts); *Ingredient X* (Royal Court Upstairs); *The Lady in the Van* (national tour); *The Herbal Bed*, *The Real Thing* (Salisbury Playhouse); *Romeo and Juliet* (Shakespeare's Globe); *Encourage the Others* (Almeida); *Doctor Faustus, Edward II, A Taste of Honey, Salt* (Royal Exchange, Manchester); *No Idea* (Improbable theatre at the Young Vic); *Some Like It Hip Hop* (Sadler's Wells).

Awards include: winner of the 2011 MEN Award for Best Design for *Doctor Faustus* at the Royal Exchange and nomination for *Salt* at the Royal Exchange Studio.

Tom Wells Writer

Theatre for the Bush includes: *Beardy* (in response to Judges as part of *Sixty-Six Books*), *Fossils* (for *Where's my Seat?*)

In 2009 he was selected for Paines Plough's Future Perfect attachment and this year he has been Associate Playwright at the Bush.

Plays include: *Me, As A Penguin* (West Yorkshire Playhouse/ Arcola); *About A Goth* (Paines Plough/Oràn Mór); *Notes for First Time Astronauts* (Paines Plough LATER at Soho); *Fossils* (Bush) and *Spacewang* (Hull Truck Theatre).

He has been co-commissioned by Paines Plough, West Yorkshire Playhouse and Hull Truck Theatre, and is writing a short film for Channel 4/Touchpaper as part of *Coming Up*.

The Bush Theatre

'These are great times for the Bush Theatre... the new building already looks like a winner' Charles Spencer, *Telegraph*

Since its inception in 1972, the Bush Theatre has pursued its singular vision of discovery, risk and entertainment from its home on the corner of Shepherds Bush Green. That vision is valued and embraced by a community of audience and artists radiating out from our distinctive corner of West London across the world. The Bush is a local theatre with an international reputation. From its beginning, the Bush has produced hundreds of groundbreaking premieres, many of them Bush commissions, and hosted guest productions by leading companies and artists from across the world. On any given night, those queuing at the foot of our stairs to take their seats could have travelled from Auckland or popped in from round the corner.

What draws them to the Bush is the promise of a good night out and our proven commitment to launch, from our stage, successive generations of playwrights and artists. Samuel Adamson, David Eldridge, Jonathan Harvey, Catherine Johnson, Tony Kushner, Stephen Poliakoff, Jack Thorne and Victoria Wood (all then unknown) began their careers at the Bush. The unwritten contract between talent and risk is understood by actors who work at the Bush, creating roles in untested new plays. Unique amongst local theatres, the Bush consistently draws actors of the highest reputation and calibre. Joseph Fiennes and Ian Hart recently took leading roles in a first play by an unknown playwright to great critical success. John Simm and Richard Wilson acted in premieres, both of which transferred into the West End. The Bush has won over 100 awards, and developed an enviable reputation for touring its acclaimed productions nationally and internationally.

Audiences and organisations far beyond our stage profit from the risks we take. The value attached to the Bush by other theatres and by the film and television industries is both significant and considerable. The Bush receives more than 3,000 scripts every year, and reads and responds to them all. This is one small part of a comprehensive playwrights' development programme which nurtures the relationship between writer and director, as well as playwright residencies and commissions. Everything that we do to develop playwrights focuses them towards a production on our stage or beyond.

We also run an ambitious education, training and professional development programme, bushfutures, providing opportunities for different sectors of the community and professionals to access the expertise of Bush playwrights, directors, designers, technicians and actors, and to play an active role in influencing the future development of the theatre and its programme. 2009 saw the launch of our new social networking and online publishing website www.bushgreen.org. The site is a great new forum for playwrights and theatre people to meet, share experiences and collaborate. Through this pioneering work, the Bush will reach and connect with new writers and new audiences, and find new plays to stage.

With this season, we have opened the doors of the new Bush Theatre. Already, the building feels like it is owned and loved by our audiences and by our artists. There are people meeting, talking and drinking coffee in the café and bar from 8 a.m. to late and the spirit of the Bush is translated into this warm and genial atmosphere. There is a bright future for the company with its new theatre and new Artistic Director, Madani Younis, who is shortly to take up his new role. This season is my last as Artistic Director and working with our fantastic team to bring the company into a new home has been an incredible experience. I hope that you will join me and those who have already been through our doors in celebrating the achievement and potential of the Bush's new home.

Josie Rourke
Artistic Director

At the Bush Theatre

Artistic Director **Josie Rourke**
Executive Director **Angela Bond**
Associate Director **Tamara Harvey**

Assistant Producer **Sade Banks**
Duty Managers **Sarah Binley, Michael Byrne**
Theatre Manager **Annette Butler**
Marketing Manager **Sophie Coke-Steel**
Digital Manager **Stacy Coyne**
Head of Individual Giving **Caroline Dyott**
Technical Manager **Neil Hobbs**
Development Administrator **Lucy Howe**
Literary Manager **Naia Johns**
General Manager **Eleanor Lang**
Head of Trusts and Foundations **Bethany Ann McDonald**
Production Manager **Anthony Newton**
Producer **Rachel Tyson**
Acting Theatre Administrator **Laura-Jane Zielinska**
& Assistant to the Directors

Associateships, Internships and Attachments

Commercial Consultant Nathalie Bristow
Composer on Attachment Michael Bruce
Bush Producing and Administrative Intern Elodie Vidal
Bush Literary Intern Scarlett Creme
Production Assistant Clay Harding
Pearson Playwright Nancy Harris**
Press Representative Kate Morley
Development Officer Leonara Twynam
Local Business Development Manager Trish Wadley
Leverhulme Trust Associate Playwright Tom Wells
Creative Associates Kate Budgen, Hannah Dickinson, Olly Hawes, Alice Lacey, Nessa Muthy
Associate Artists Tanya Burns, Arthur Darvill, Chloe Emmerson, James Farncombe, Richard Jordan, Emma Laxton, Paul Miller, Lucy Osborne
Front of House Assistants Benedict Adiyemi, Chrissy Angus, Devante Anglin, Lily Beck, Gemma Bergomi, Tom Brewer, Nathan Byron, Simone Finney, Aaron Gordon, Amy Hydes, Michael McBride, Ava Morgan, Hannah Smith, Chloe Stephens, Gareth Walker
Duty Technicians Ben Ainsley, Simon Perkins, Chris Withers

* **Bold** indicates full-time staff; regular indicates part-time/temporary.
** Sponsored by the Peggy Ramsay Foundation Award as part of the Pearson Playwrights' scheme
*** Sponsored by Kingston University School of Humanities through a Knowledge Transfer Partnership

The Bush Theatre, 7 Uxbridge Road, London, W12 8LJ
Box Office: 020 8743 5050 Administration: 020 8743 3584 email: info@bushtheatre.co.uk
The Alternative Theatre Company Ltd (The Bush Theatre) is a registered charity and a company limited by guarantee. Registered in England No. 1221968. Charity No. 270080

supported by
hammersmith & fulham

Supported by
ARTS COUNCIL ENGLAND

Be there at the beginning

The Bush Theatre would like to say a very special 'Thank You' to the following patrons, corporate sponsors and trusts and foundations, whose valuable contributions continue to help us nurture, develop and present some of the brightest new literary stars and theatre artists.

Lone Star
Gianni Alen-Buckley
Michael Alen-Buckley
Jonathan Ford
   & Susannah Herbert
Catherine Johnson
Caryn Mandabach
Miles Morland
Lady Susie Sainsbury
John & Tita Shakeshaft
Nicholas Whyatt

Handful of Stars
Anonymous
Micaela & Chris Boas
Jim Broadbent
Sarah Cooke
Clyde Cooper
Blake & Michael Daffey
David and Alexandra Emmerson
Catherine Faulks*
Chris and Sofia Fenichell
Christopher Hampton
Douglas Kennedy
Mark & Sophie Lewisohn
Adrian & Antonia Lloyd
Mounzer & Beatriz Nasr
Georgia Oetker
Claudia Rossler
Naomi Russell
Eva Sanchez-Ampudia
   & Cyrille Walter
Joana & Henrik Schliemann*
Larus Shields

Rising Stars
Anonymous
Tessa Bamford
David Bernstein
   & Sophie Caruth
John Bottrill
David Brooks
Maggie Burrows
Clive Butler
Matthew Byam Shaw
Benedetta Cassinelli
Tim & Andrea Clark
Judy Cummins
   & Karen Doherty
Matthew Cushen
Irene Danilovich
Michael & Marianne de Giorgio
Yvonna Demczynska
Ruth East
Jane & David Fletcher
Lady Antonia Fraser
Vivien Goodwin
Sarah Griffin

Hugh & Sarah Grootenhuis
Sarah Hall
Hugo & Julia Heath
Roy Hillyard
Urs & Alice Hodler
Bea Hollond
Simon Johnson
Davina & Malcom Judelson
Paul & Cathy Kafka
Rupert Jolley & Aine Kelly
Tarek & Diala Khlat
Heather Killen
Sue Knox
Neil LaBute
Eugenie White
   & Andrew Loewenthal
Isabella Macpherson
Peter & Bettina Mallinson
Charlie & Polly McAndrew
Michael McCoy
Judith Mellor
Roger Miall
David & Anita Miles
Caro Millington
Pedro & Carole Neuhaus
Kate Pakenham
Mark Paterson
Judith & Amanda Platt
Radfin Courier Service
Kirsty Raper
Clare Rich
Sarah Richards
Damian Rourke
Jon & NoraLee Sedmak
Russ Shaw & Lesley Hill
Brian Smith
Nick Starr
The Uncertainty Principle
The van Tulleken family
Francois
   & Arelle von Hurter
Trish Wadley
Amanda Waggott
Olivia Warham
Edward Wild
Peter Wilson-Smith & Kat Callo
Alison Winter

Bush Club
Hardeep Kalsi
Jonny Maitland
Simon Meadon
John & Jacqui Pearson
Mark Roberts
Alexander Russell
John & Joanna Trotter
Rosalind Wyllie

Corporate Sponsors
Spotlight Supporter
John Lewis, Park Royal

Footlight Supporter
The Agency (London) Ltd

Lightbulb Supporters
AKA
Curtis Brown Group Ltd
Mozzo Coffee & La Marzocco

The Bush would also like to thank **Markson Pianos**, **Westfield** and **West 12 Shopping & Leisure Centre** for in-kind support, and **UBS** for their sponsorship of Supporters' evenings.

Trusts and Foundations
The Andrew Lloyd Webber
   Foundation
The Daisy Trust
The D'Oyly Carte Charitable
   Trust
EC&O Venues Charitable Trust
The Elizabeth & Gordon Bloor
   Charitable Foundation
Foundation for Sport & the Arts
Garfield Weston Foundation
Garrick Charitable Trust
The Gatsby Charitable
   Foundation
The Goldsmiths' Company
The Harold Hyam Wingate
   Foundation
Jerwood Charitable Foundation
The John Thaw Foundation
The King James Bible Trust
The Laurie & Gillian Marsh
   Charitable Trust
The Leverhulme Trust
The Martin Bowley Charitable
   Trust
The Hon M J Samuel Charitable
   Trust
Sir Siegmund Warburg's
   Voluntary Settlement

THE KITCHEN SINK

Tom Wells

For my mum and dad, with love

'I write this sitting in the kitchen sink.'

Dodie Smith

Characters

MARTIN
KATH
SOPHIE
BILLY
PETE

This text went to press before the end of rehearsals and so may differ slightly from the play as performed.

SPRING

1

A shabby kitchen. Peeling paint. Scruffy lino. Table, chairs, cupboards, cooker, sink.

KATH *is chopping vegetables with her back to* BILLY. *Still in her dinner-lady overalls – they were already covered in food so she might as well be.*

A bit of a milk float is on the kitchen table, leaking oil onto one of her best tea towels.

BILLY *is sitting at the kitchen table, examining his portrait of Dolly Parton. In the portrait, Dolly is smiling, wearing a blue dress which is tight and quite revealing. It is a good portrait though.*

BILLY. What d'you think about the nipples? Mum?

> KATH *doesn't respond.*

Mum, can you look please? Mum? Mum?

> KATH *stops chopping vegetables and turns round.*

KATH. Sorry, love?

BILLY. The nipples? Dolly Parton's. What d'you think?

> KATH *looks.*

KATH. Oh, they're lovely, Billy. Spot on.

> KATH *turns to carry on with her vegetables.* BILLY *looks at the portrait again.*

BILLY. You don't think they're too much?

> KATH *smiles.* BILLY *looks troubled.*

KATH. No.

BILLY. I'm worried she looks a bit cheap though.

KATH. Don't be daft, Billy. Just looks like Dolly Parton. On a cold day.

BILLY. I did imagine it being cold.

BILLY *thinks for a moment*.

What about sequins?

KATH *doesn't answer. She's looking for a casserole dish*.

Mum? Mum?

KATH. What, love?

BILLY. Will you look?

KATH. I'm trying to get on with your dad's tea really.

BILLY. Just look though.

KATH *looks*.

KATH. What's the matter?

BILLY. What about sequins?

KATH *frowns*.

KATH. Actually on the nipples?

BILLY. No just in general. I got these blue ones but. I'm not sure if they'll help or, you know. Hinder.

KATH. You must do what you think, love.

BILLY. That's the thing though: at the moment I think it looks good, but then it might look better with sequins. They might sort of, lift it a bit.

KATH *goes back to chopping her vegetables*.

KATH. Okay.

BILLY. Or they might ruin it and I won't have time to fix it before tomorrow. So maybe it's better to play it safe.

KATH. Mm.

BILLY. But then, what if I get there tomorrow and they say, 'we do like this portrait of Dolly Parton, it's technically a good portrait, looks like her and everything but: we feel she's lacking something.'

KATH *pops a bit of carrot in her mouth.*

KATH. Like a bra?

BILLY. No, Mum, like her spirit.

KATH. Right then. Right. Decision made.

BILLY. Definitely. Definitely sequins.

KATH *goes back to her carrots.* BILLY *looks at the portrait, a bit crestfallen.*

Thing is though, with sequins.

KATH. I don't really have time for this, Billy.

BILLY. But I just think, you know –

KATH. I'm behind with your dad's tea.

BILLY. Sort of think –

KATH. Thought if I had it ready.

BILLY. I'm just quite worried though.

KATH. For when he gets back.

BILLY. You're not even listening.

KATH (*a touch impatient*). It's a sodding picture, Billy. Of Dolly Parton. How hard can it be?

Silence.

BILLY *is hurt.*

KATH *breathes out slowly. She stops chopping vegetables. She turns around.*

Sorry. I shouldn't've.

BILLY. No, you're. You're right. It is a sodding picture. Of Dolly Parton.

I'm fucked.

KATH. Billy…

BILLY. Doesn't matter.

KATH. I think it looks lovely. Honest it does. Really lovely.

BILLY *manages a smile*.

BILLY. Cheers.

KATH. And I mean, I don't even know anything about art so. They're sure to like it more.

BILLY *looks troubled*.

BILLY. Mm.

KATH. All your other stuff as well. Them photos of clouds, that film of Edna dancing to, thingy.

BILLY. Justin Timberlake.

KATH. You'll be a shoo-in. You will.

BILLY. You think?

KATH. Come here.

KATH *gives* BILLY *a reassuring hug*.

Whatever happens, it'll be alright.

BILLY. Hope so.

BILLY *looks at the portrait again*.

Still think I'll give the sequins a miss.

KATH. I'd better get on.

She does.

BILLY *goes to the sink. Peers into its depths. Sniffs*.

BILLY. I can still smell it, Mum.

KATH. Just keep plunging, it'll…

He picks up a plunger. Half-heartedly plunges.

BILLY. D'you not think we ought to get it sorted though? Properly. Mum?

KATH *takes the plunger off* BILLY. *She plunges, vigorously*.

KATH. Think I'd miss it. Quite therapeutic really, a good plunge. D'you want to set the table?

KATH *goes back to her vegetables.*

BILLY *leans the portrait against the table leg on the floor, gets some cutlery and stops.*

He is wondering what to do about the bit of milk float.

BILLY. Um, shall I move this?

KATH. What's up, love?

BILLY. What shall I do about…?

KATH. Oh, just leave it there.

BILLY. Sure?

KATH. Positive.

BILLY *takes a moment. The penny drops.*

BILLY. Is this a special tea, Mum?

KATH. Sorry, love.

BILLY. A special tea.

KATH. Not really, casserole, why?

BILLY. Nothing just. You seem to be putting quite a lot of energy into those carrots. So I wondered if maybe it was, you know. A special tea. To talk about…

BILLY *looks at the bit of milk float.*

KATH. It might come up.

BILLY. Right. Maybe just set it for you and Dad then. The table.

KATH. Anything, Billy, just.

KATH *carries on with her carrots.*

SOPHIE *comes into the kitchen from outside. She is wearing her ju-jitsu gear and carrying a holdall. She sees the portrait.*

SOPHIE. Frigging hell. Nice nipples, Billy.

BILLY. What?

SOPHIE. Just saying sort of. God, they're a bit. Erect.

SOPHIE *gestures towards the portrait.* BILLY *looks downcast.*

BILLY. Cheers.

KATH. How did it go tonight, love?

SOPHIE. Oh, you know.

KATH. Girls alright?

SOPHIE. Yeah. Good I think. I mean, it's a mixture really, all these sort of proper tough cookies, and then like: weepers. But, you know. Think I'm getting through to them. Some good blocking today. Not so many bruises. Sensei Steve seemed pleased.

Trying to sound casual.

Said he'll put me in for my black belt in the summer so. You know.

BILLY. Soph, that's amazing!

KATH. That's brilliant, love.

SOPHIE *shrugs.*

Isn't it?

SOPHIE. Reckon I'll fuck it up to be honest. I do that.

KATH. Come on, Soph, course you won't.

SOPHIE *(firmly).* Smells nice.

KATH *goes back to her vegetables.*

BILLY. It's a special tea.

SOPHIE. Oh, cos of…

SOPHIE *indicates the lump of milk float.* BILLY *nods.*

I'm off out anyway.

KATH. You've only just got in.

SOPHIE. Well, you know.

KATH. Somewhere nice?

SOPHIE. Think we're off into Hull.

KATH. Very nice.

All of you going?

SOPHIE. Not really.

She sits down on the floor and looks at the picture close up.

You nervous?

BILLY. Bit nervous.

SOPHIE. Definitely taking that though?

BILLY. I am yeah.

SOPHIE *looks worried.*

SOPHIE. But, I mean, you've got other stuff?

BILLY. Bits and bobs. Them photos I took of clouds.

KATH. Edna bringing sexy back.

BILLY. This is my main piece though. Took me ages so I thought…

SOPHIE. Right.

BILLY. What d'you mean?

SOPHIE. Nothing, just. They can be quite snobby and that can't they?

BILLY. I don't get you.

SOPHIE. I just wonder what they'll think, sitting in their little office in London surrounded by all Leonardo da Vincis and that. Tracey Emin. You turn up from Withernsea with Dolly Parton tucked under your arm. Except her nipples won't fit.

KATH. Sophie.

SOPHIE. I'm kidding. You'll be fine.

KATH *goes to the cupboard and rummages through a box of things in packets.*

BILLY *picks up the portrait and really looks at it.*

BILLY. Soph's right though. They will look down on Dolly.
People do.

But then I just think, she's properly inspiring, isn't she? And
she's got this habit of sort of. At key moments in my life just.
Like I remember the first time I heard her – Year Eight
school trip. To the abbatoir. Got on the coach and all the lads
were having a go at the driver cos they wanted to listen to
sort of, 'Bangin' Tunes '03' or whatever, and he just: ignored
them. Carried on listening to his music. I couldn't believe
anyone could just ignore them and carry on. Cos they gave
me quite a hard time and that. All the time really. So I started
listening too. And it was 'Jolene'. And, you know, it's just.
Someone just singing the whole of themselves, all their
fragile bits and their needy bits and making it, beautiful, I
dunno, strong or, not giving a shit who hears it sort of. So I
thought it'd be nice if she was there with me tomorrow. Cos
it's. Think I'm putting a bit of myself on the line or
something. Quite a lot of myself really. Dreams and that.

BILLY *stops for a moment. Nobody is listening.*

This time next week I'll know.

2

KATH *and* MARTIN *sit facing each other at the table.*

KATH *is looking at* MARTIN. MARTIN *is looking at his plate,
underwhelmed. He looks up.*

MARTIN. Couscous?

KATH. I made it with lemon.

MARTIN. Oh right, is it… What is it?

KATH. It's sort of, it's Moroccan I think.

MARTIN *lifts a bit of couscous onto his fork. Lets it drop.*

MARTIN. Looks like dust.

KATH. Everything else is just what you're used to. Casserole.

KATH *sighs*.

Don't eat it then.

MARTIN. Feels a bit funny without potatoes.

KATH. I thought maybe it was time for a change.

MARTIN. Definitely a change.

KATH. Thought we could have a nice sit-down and a chat and everything.

MARTIN. Oh.

KATH. Just a nice meal, bit of couscous.

MARTIN. Fine, fine. We'll do that.

KATH. Also:

KATH *moves the lump of milk float in front of* MARTIN.

Think we need to talk about your milk float.

MARTIN *sighs, tucks into his couscous*.

Martin?

MARTIN. Don't want to talk about it.

KATH. Pardon?

MARTIN. Just want to eat my tea.

KATH *looks surprised*.

If that's alright.

KATH *sighs*.

What?

KATH. Nothing just. I do wonder if you're pushing it a bit today, Martin.

MARTIN *droops*.

Right.

KATH grabs MARTIN's plate, stands up and holds it over the bin. He has a fork full of couscous in his hand. It stays there, hovering.

MARTIN. What're you doing that for?

KATH. Why d'you think?

MARTIN. Please give me my tea back, Kath. Please.

KATH. Talk to me then.

MARTIN. I'll talk to you when I've had my tea.

KATH. You'll talk to me now or you won't have any tea. Be eating out the bin.

MARTIN (*sadly*). Might as well be. Bloody, Africa dust.

KATH. There's people going hungry, Martin.

MARTIN. Yes. Cos you've nicked the couscous.

KATH. Don't tempt me.

MARTIN. Kath.

KATH. I'll do it, Martin, I will. I'm this close.

MARTIN. It's slipping.

KATH. Good.

All the same, KATH puts the plate level.

A moment.

MARTIN. Are you alright, love?

KATH. No I'm not actually. I'm worried.

MARTIN. You're always worried. Can I have my tea?

KATH. Billy's got his interview tomorrow –

MARTIN. Tomorrow? Thought it was –

KATH. Seems to think he can turn up with Dolly Parton in a tight top, they'll welcome him with open arms. I mean I don't have the first clue what they're looking for but. He's not got a Plan B and I just... Don't know what's going on with Soph, barely talks to me. I keep hoping she'll grow out of it but she's, you know, she's twenty-one.

MARTIN. Soph's alright.

KATH. I don't think she is, Martin. I think she's unhappy. I think something's really wrong and we just go 'Soph's alright' and, you know… And you.

MARTIN. What you on about 'me'?

KATH. Every time the phone rings it's someone bloody cancelling.

MARTIN. That's not true.

KATH. Mostly is.

MARTIN. Sometimes they're lactose intolerant.

KATH. Well, I don't believe that for a second. I've seen Debbie Speck buying Müller Rice.

MARTIN. Can't help any of that.

KATH. I know, I know, but it happens and, and then I have to tell you and. Three this week, it's only Tuesday.

MARTIN. It's Wednesday, love.

KATH. That's not… The point is: your milk float's knackered. This bit – what's this? Is it important? Cos it has quite clearly fallen off, Martin. It has quite clearly dropped off. And I know you can't always be going backwards and forwards to the garage but I'm not sure masking tape's the solution. I'm really not.

MARTIN. I can look after my own milk float.

KATH. Really?

MARTIN. Yes, God's sake: I took it off to clean it. The tape's to, you can write on it, remind me what goes where. I'll put it back after tea.

A moment. MARTIN *smiles.*

If I ever get my tea.

KATH *smiles, but is still worried.*

KATH. No, Martin, don't.

MARTIN. Come on, love. It's getting cold. My couscous.

KATH. Just, listen, a second.

MARTIN. I'm hungry.

KATH. One minute. One minute of your time. Because, I mean, this isn't the first, this isn't the first bit of milk float to appear on my kitchen table. You're getting through my tea towels at an alarming rate and, I'm right about it falling to bits, I've heard what it sounds like when you go over a speed bump. I'm right about those people cancelling. Soph's only helping you till she gets her black belt – you'll be stuck then.

MARTIN. What are you saying, Kath?

Deep breath.

KATH. I'm saying: it feels like time for a change. A big decision. Can't always be…

KATH *indicates the bit of milk float.*

That's what I think, anyway.

Silence.

MARTIN. Come sit down, love.

KATH *does. She's a bit defeated.*

KATH. D'you want this back?

MARTIN. I wouldn't mind.

KATH *puts the plate back down in front of* MARTIN.

KATH. Sorry about the bin and that.

MARTIN. Sorry about the phone calls. But you have to…

It'll pick up, in the summer.

KATH. There's Tescos though.

MARTIN. We've got a new range. Yogurts.

KATH. Tescos have yogurts. And that's only. You can't pin your future on yogurts.

MARTIN. I don't know what else I can do.

KATH. There's lots of things you can do.

MARTIN. Like what?

KATH *thinks*.

KATH (*lightly*). Lots of things.

MARTIN. I'm a milkman, Kath. I do milkmanly things.

KATH. I've been a dinner lady for twenty-five years. I've cooked chips every day for twenty-five years. Doesn't stop me doing other things.

MARTIN *looks at his couscous*.

MARTIN. No.

A moment.

KATH *laughs*. MARTIN *smiles*.

Just hang on for the summer, eh? We'll be back on track by then. Holidaymakers. The caravan site. I promise.

KATH *doesn't answer*.

BILLY *comes in*.

Alright, Billy?

BILLY. Yeah, good thanks, just looking for…

BILLY *finds the sequins*.

Cos I thought I'd leave the nipples showing through her dress sort of, but then I was looking at it and I was like: Billy, you absolute idiot, that's a terrible idea. But I don't have time to paint over them now – cos it's oils and that – so I thought if I covered her dress in sequins, just covered it completely, be just as good. Before, you know. And also I can call it collage then, or something. Mixed media.

MARTIN *looks bewildered*.

You alright?

A moment.

MARTIN. Fine, I think.

Silence.

They don't know how to talk to each other.

BILLY. How was tea?

MARTIN. Fine, yeah, wasn't it, Kath? Yeah it was…

KATH. It was special.

3

The kitchen is empty. SOPHIE *arrives back with* PETE.
PETE *hovers in the doorway.*

SOPHIE. Are you coming in or?

PETE. I wasn't sure.

SOPHIE. Right. Well. If you make your mind up, let me know.

PETE *nods.*

I'm having a cup of tea, do you want one?

SOPHIE *fills the kettle. The water splutters a bit.*

PETE. Please yeah.

Actually, it's quite late isn't it? It's got quite a lot of caffeine
in, tea. My gran says there's no wonder I can't sleep,
drinking all this tea late at night. She has Horlicks instead. I
tried it once but. Made me gag.

SOPHIE. So that's a no?

PETE. No thanks.

SOPHIE. I won't tell your gran.

PETE *thinks about it. Smiles. Nods.*

PETE. Bit naughty.

SOPHIE. You'll have to sit down.

PETE. I'm alright here.

SOPHIE. Thing is, Pete: it's quite weird.

PETE. Oh, yeah.

He comes in. He doesn't sit down yet though. Hovers, awkwardly. Picks up a potato masher. Examines it.

SOPHIE. What are you doing now?

PETE. Just, you know.

SOPHIE. Sit down.

PETE. Sorry.

Silence.

Sink's still bunged up is it? I can have a look if you –

SOPHIE. It's fine.

Pause.

PETE. Your kettle's quite a slow boiler.

SOPHIE. Pete, why are you doing this?

PETE. I'm not.

SOPHIE. You're being weird.

PETE. It is quite slow. For a kettle.

SOPHIE. Stop it.

PETE. Sorry. Sorry.

SOPHIE. Stop saying –

PETE. Sorry, I know. What a knob.

SOPHIE. Pete.

PETE. Feel like I've cocked tonight up really. A bit. Cocked it all up.

SOPHIE. Right.

PETE. I wanted it to be. I wanted it to be.

SOPHIE. What?

PETE. Sort of, dashing or something. But it's hard, isn't it, on a moped? It's only till I finish my training.

SOPHIE. Yep. Then you're getting a van.

PETE. And the food. Shit. I asked Danny where was good in town cos I don't go in that much, not to the middle. He said there but, looking back, and that's the thing with Danny isn't it, he does take the piss, a lot.

SOPHIE. It was alright.

PETE. I didn't think much to it.

SOPHIE. Think it was quite good for, you know for. For Nando's.

PETE. And then being back here and, you know, drinking tea or –

SOPHIE. If it's tea that's the problem, you don't have to.

PETE. No.

SOPHIE. I mean it's good tea but.

PETE. Milky.

SOPHIE. You like it milky.

PETE. Yep.

SOPHIE. You do though.

PETE. Lovely.

SOPHIE. Said that's how they make it in Preston.

PETE. Cheers.

SOPHIE. There's biscuits somewhere.

PETE. It's alright thanks. I'm still suffering a bit from. Still quite full.

SOPHIE. Is that why you're being weird? The peri-peri chicken.

PETE. I just felt a bit out of my comfort zone.

SOPHIE *smiles*.

SOPHIE. Such a div.

PETE. But I mean, not just that. I think – oh, I dunno.

SOPHIE. What?

PETE. Sounds a bit stupid out loud.

SOPHIE. Can't wait.

PETE. S'pose I'm just, I'm not a hundred per cent sure if, I mean, I just wanted to check: was this a, or, cos there were moments when, you know, it did feel like a sort of, but then there were other times when, like: you did call me pathetic quite a lot. And tried to set me up with your brother. Twice.

SOPHIE. I just think you'd make a lovely couple.

PETE. Reckon Billy might prefer someone who's, you know. Actually gay.

SOPHIE. Yeah maybe.

SOPHIE smiles. PETE does too.

Bit weird without the others isn't it?

PETE. Mm.

Be alright though.

SOPHIE. You think?

PETE nods.

PETE. Yeah, course it will, course.

He looks at her for quite a long time. About to do something. Not sure.

Um, should we…?

SOPHIE. What?

PETE. No, I mean, just thinking: maybe it'd help to, if we, just, get it out the way, the big, the, the you know the…

A vulnerable moment for SOPHIE. As if she'd quite like to.

…um, the…

But no. She looks down into her mug. Sad.

SOPHIE. Not tonight, Pete.

A moment.

PETE. Oh.

SOPHIE. Maybe just drink your tea.

PETE *looks a bit hurt.*

PETE. Yeah. Course.

Drinks his tea. Swallows.

Quick, before my gran finds out.

Laughs. Stops laughing.

A moment.

SOPHIE *softens.*

SOPHIE. How is she?

PETE. Sorry?

SOPHIE. How's Edna?

PETE. Yeah she's, um. Fine I think, yeah.

A moment.

I mean, she's not amazing.

SOPHIE. But she's alright though?

PETE *shrugs.*

Struggling?

PETE *nods.*

PETE. Bit yeah. No.

SOPHIE. What's up?

PETE. Nothing.

SOPHIE. Sure?

PETE. Mm.

SOPHIE. Pete?

PETE. It's fine, I'm being. Shouldn't've said anything.

SOPHIE. You haven't said anything.

PETE. No but.

SOPHIE. Fuck's sake, Pete, out with it.

PETE *sighs. He tells this story to his mug.*

PETE. Just, the other day, Thursday, I came home a bit early, she was sat in the front room looking a bit. She was watching *Eggheads* and, I dunno. Sounds daft but. There was this. Smelt like she'd been smoking, you know. Well, yeah, smoking...

PETE*'s eyes widen.* SOPHIE*'s too.*

SOPHIE. No.

PETE. It's fine, I'm being.

SOPHIE. Bloody hell, Pete.

PETE. Don't, don't. Shouldn't've said anything. Cos it can help can't it? With, less painful and that so. And I don't want her to be in any sort of. Suppose I should just.

SOPHIE*'s trying not to laugh.*

It's not funny, Soph.

SOPHIE. No.

PETE. You've got a mum and dad and... I've only got my gran.

SOPHIE. I know.

PETE. Worry about her.

SOPHIE. Course you do. Course.

A moment.

I mean: it is a gateway drug.

PETE *smiles. Looks up.*

PETE. Sod off.

SOPHIE *smiles. Reaches across. Holds his elbow. Just for a moment.*

4

KATH *and* BILLY *have wooden spoons.* BILLY *is poised by the CD player. A letter is open on the table.*

BILLY. Ready?

KATH. Hang on.

She clears her throat. Smiles.

Ready.

BILLY *makes an excited noise, presses play. The introduction to Dolly Parton's 'Tennessee Homesick Blues'.* BILLY *counts* KATH *in.*

KATH *yodels the first yodel.*

BILLY. Brilliant.

KATH. Your go.

BILLY *yodels the second yodel.*

BILLY *sings the words.* KATH *doesn't know the words. He hands her the album sleeve, with lyrics. She gets quite into it.*

For the chorus they stand on chairs. For the next yodel, BILLY *is on the table.*

MARTIN *stomps in, obviously recently awake, turns the CD off, and begins to stomp out.*

What you doing? Martin?

MARTIN. Shut. Up.

KATH. Martin, what's?

MARTIN. Trying to have ten minutes.

KATH. Come back here a sec.

MARTIN. Trying to sleep.

KATH. No just quickly, Billy's got something to –

BILLY. Mum, it's fine.

KATH. Billy's got something to –

MARTIN. Can it wait? I've been up since four.

KATH. Martin, I'm trying to –

   MARTIN *reappears*.

MARTIN. What? What is it?

   A moment.

BILLY (*downcast*). Nothing, doesn't matter.

MARTIN. What you doing on the table?

KATH. Martin.

BILLY. Nothing, just. You know.

   BILLY *gets down*.

KATH. We're celebrating, love.

MARTIN. What?

KATH (*encouraging*). Tell him then.

   BILLY *shrugs*.

   Go on.

MARTIN. Come on then.

BILLY. Um it's. Got into college so. The London one so. Yeah.
   That's it really.

   BILLY *hands him the letter.*

   Just came now.

MARTIN. Oh. Right.

BILLY. Didn't know you were. Thought you were.

MARTIN. That's alright, that's.

   MARTIN *looks at the letter. Nods*.

   Right.

   Are you pleased then?

BILLY. What d'you mean?

MARTIN. Are you pleased?

BILLY. Um. Yeah?

KATH. He's up on the table yodelling, Martin, course he's pleased.

MARTIN. Well, I don't know do I?

KATH. Been wanting this for years. It's really good.

MARTIN. Alright.

A moment.

Good on you, Billy. Good on you.

A moment. BILLY *was hoping for a more enthusiastic response.*

D'you want thingy back on?

BILLY. You're alright, Dad. I better… anyway.

KATH. Billy –

BILLY. Nah, Mum, it's…

BILLY *picks up his letter. Goes upstairs.*

KATH *looks at* MARTIN, *who is yawning.*

MARTIN. What?

KATH. I think you might need to be a bit more supportive, Martin.

MARTIN. Oh for –

KATH. Martin.

MARTIN. I said well done.

KATH. You didn't, love. You didn't.

MARTIN. Well, I meant it. I meant well done.

KATH. Say it then.

MARTIN *sighs.*

MARTIN. I'm going back to sleep.

SUMMER

5

The portrait of Dolly Parton (with sequins) is on the wall.

KATH *and* BILLY *are drying up.* PETE *has arrived with some slightly forlorn flowers. He looks at them, a bit bemused.*

PETE. Don't know why I bought them really.

KATH. Don't say that, Pete.

PETE. I don't.

KATH. I think it's lovely to see a bit of romance.

PETE. Oh, it isn't –

KATH. D'you know what I got for Valentine's Day this year?

BILLY. Mum, you need to let go of this. It's July.

KATH. D'you know what I got, Pete?

> PETE *shakes his head.*

A chainsaw.

> PETE *doesn't know what to say.*

PETE. Crikey.

BILLY. In fairness: you did ask for a surprise.

KATH. Meant Thorntons, Billy. Nice day out.

> Got Martin a, this little jar of chocolate body paint.

> We just had it on toast.

PETE. These are more sort of 'well done' than… But I haven't, haven't heard.

KATH. They're later back than I thought.

PETE. You haven't –

> KATH *shakes her head.*

KATH. Martin's not answering his phone. We daren't ring Soph in case it goes off in the middle of a move.

KATH *looks at the flowers as if they might not make it.*

Might just pop these in a bit of water, see if we can perk them up a bit.

KATH *goes to the sink but struggles with the tap.*

PETE. D'you want me to have a...

KATH *smacks the top of the tap with a hammer. It turns easily. She fills a vase with water and plonks the flowers in.*

KATH. There we go. Hot drink?

PETE. I'm fine thanks.

KATH. Are you sure? Putting the kettle on anyway.

PETE *considers. Smiles.*

PETE. Cup of tea'd be lovely, thanks.

KATH. Sit down then, love.

PETE *sits down.*

There's muffins if you fancy.

PETE. I'm alright.

BILLY. New recipe, Pete – (*Smiling.*) courgette.

PETE *tries not to laugh.*

KATH *tries to fill the kettle. The tap won't work. She picks up the hammer.*

PETE. I can have a look at that, if you...

KATH. You sit down. Must get sick of.

KATH *hits the tap again.*

PETE. Just, I'm not sure that helps.

KATH. Probably not, no, but it does me the world of good.

KATH *hits the tap with a hammer.*

One day I'm just going to rip the whole lot out and...

KATH *hits the tap hard and it starts to leak out of the side.*

Bugger.

PETE. Never mind it's, um. Easily done. With a hammer. I've got a few things with me so...

PETE *empties a selection of tools from various pockets.*

BILLY (*looking out of the window*). They're back.

KATH *goes to the door.* PETE *picks up the flowers.*

KATH. Oh thank God. I've actually been quite...

SOPHIE *barges in, past her mum, past* PETE *and away.*

Soph, what's –

SOPHIE. Don't, alright. Just, don't.

SOPHIE *disappears.* PETE *looks at the flowers, crestfallen.*

Doors slam upstairs.

PETE *puts the flowers down and goes back to the tap.*

KATH. You alright up there? Soph?!

MARTIN *appears in the doorway.*

What's happened?

MARTIN *sighs.*

Soph!?

MARTIN. I wouldn't, love.

KATH. Has it gone alright?

MARTIN *pulls a face.*

MARTIN. Two guesses.

KATH. But she's got her black belt though?

MARTIN *shakes his head.*

Shit. Shitty shitty bollocks. You were gone that long we thought you must be, celebrating or...

MARTIN *laughs.*

What's happened then?

MARTIN *sits down*.

MARTIN. We've been to casualty.

BILLY. What?

KATH. What are you on about, casualty?

MARTIN. Casualty. Casualty.

KATH. Who's been to? God, was it Soph? (*Shouting*.) Sophie!

MARTIN. Not Soph. Soph's fine. The thingy. Examiner bloke.

KATH. What?

The tap makes a noise.

MARTIN. Oh hiya, Pete, you alright?

PETE. Fine thanks, yeah. I mean: we're all just a bit anxious about you and Soph to be honest.

MARTIN. Yep, sorry about that. Slight, um. I would've rung but I didn't have my phone. I thought I did, and I tried to text but turned out it was the remote control. Didn't have my glasses either so it took a while to dawn on me. Still. All fine now.

KATH. Apart from the man, presumably. Examiner.

MARTIN. Oh, he's alright. Once the bleeding stopped and everything. Just the swelling and that. They don't think it's broken but it's hard with noses isn't it? Hard to tell.

KATH. I still don't understand.

MARTIN. Thing is, it's not really. Should probably let Soph tell you.

PETE. Perhaps I could go up and see if she's alright? Or, somebody could.

MARTIN. I wouldn't do that, Pete. She's um. You know.

KATH. She's what? I still don't know what's happened?

MARTIN *sighs*.

MARTIN. Best to let Soph tell it really.

KATH. Well, Soph's not here.

MARTIN. Wait then.

KATH. Martin.

MARTIN. Sorry, Kath, but. I don't want to sort of. It's all quite, you know, it's quite…

SOPHIE *appears in the doorway.*

SOPHIE. I smacked him.

KATH. What? Smacked who?

SOPHIE. The examiner. Keith.

KATH. You punched him?

SOPHIE. Yeah.

KATH. What – as part of the…?

SOPHIE *shakes her head.*

Oh.

You just… You punched him?

SOPHIE. Yep. Twice as it goes. That's what did it I think, concussion-wise.

KATH. Sophie, why on earth did you…

SOPHIE. Dunno really. He's a prick.

KATH. But he must've…

SOPHIE *shrugs.*

MARTIN. Tell your mum.

SOPHIE. No.

MARTIN. Tell her.

SOPHIE. Shut up, Dad.

MARTIN. She's worried about you.

KATH. Did he hurt you?

SOPHIE. No, course not.

KATH. If he has laid a finger –

SOPHIE *(quickly).* He hasn't.

A moment.

He just.

It's.

She sighs.

He called me feisty.

A moment.

KATH. I don't...

SOPHIE. Feisty. Feisty. Over and over again.

KATH. So you punched him?

SOPHIE. Yes!

God, knew you wouldn't get it.

KATH. I just.

SOPHIE. There was three of us, right, me and these two lads
from bloody, Burton Pidsea, and he was chatting with them
beforehand, taking the piss, I could hear him, and they were
laughing like dickhead-lad laughing and then we got up and
he, I dunno. Made me go last and every time I finished he'd
just be like: 'very feisty'. Like a fucking. And I was getting
more and more. The lads were pissing themselves and Sensei
Steve was there watching, not saying anything just, and then
we finished and he, Keith, examiner whatever turned to the
lads and went: 'Bit feisty this one, eh, lads?' And I'd done,
everything right. I'd, I'd done everything I needed for my
black belt and you know, proved myself and still he was. He
wouldn't've said it about a lad. He wouldn't've taken the piss
out of... So anyway I just lost it, turned round and fucking...

But yeah. Bit of a shit day. As it goes.

And Sensei Steve was sat there gobsmacked. Sort of,
ashamed or. I dunno. It wasn't...

KATH. Oh, love.

KATH *tries to give* SOPHIE *a hug.* SOPHIE *pulls back from
it.*

SOPHIE. It's fine, Mum.

KATH. We can go round there now and. Or ring up. Sensei
Steve.

SOPHIE. It's fine just. You know. I'm a brown belt. Keith's a prick.

KATH *thinks for a minute*.

KATH. You did the right thing, love.

SOPHIE. I didn't.

A moment.

Still. Dad took him to get checked over and that just in case. I stayed in the car park. That's it. That's today.

Nobody knows what to say.

PETE. Um. Tap's mended, if you…

PETE *turns the tap on and off*.

KATH. Oh thanks, Pete, that's.

PETE. I mean, only patched up really but.

PETE *ducks under the sink for a look*.

Quite a lot of this looks a bit last-legsy to be honest. Needs replacing.

KATH. Don't worry, Pete.

KATH *shows* PETE *a big jar containing a small layer of twenty-pence coins*.

Saving up. Cos you don't miss them do you, 20ps?

PETE. No I. I suppose not.

A moment.

KATH *touches the flowers in the vase. Looks at* PETE *looking at* SOPHIE. *Makes a decision.*

KATH. Martin, have you got something to be…?

MARTIN. What's up, love?

KATH. Outside, have you? Do you need a hand with your, with your?

MARTIN. You're alright, no rush.

KATH. No let's. We'll crack on.

MARTIN. Oh.

KATH. Shall we?

MARTIN (*a bit confused*). Right.

MARTIN gets up and wanders out. KATH gives BILLY a look.

BILLY. I might go and. Do some. Art.

KATH and BILLY leave.

SOPHIE is restless. She starts looking through the kitchen drawer.

A moment.

PETE. You alright, Soph?

SOPHIE. Course I'm not fucking alright.

PETE looks indecisive for a moment. He picks up the flowers.

PETE. Um. Brought these, don't know if.

SOPHIE stops for a moment. Looks.

Danny said get yellow ones cos: non-committal.

SOPHIE. D'you always do what Danny says?

PETE. Um. Yeah?

PETE tries to give SOPHIE the flowers.

SOPHIE. Don't, Pete.

A moment.

SOPHIE goes back to the kitchen drawer.

PETE. Just leave them here then.

He lays them on the table.

SOPHIE. Take them for your gran.

PETE. Nah, Soph. Get some others for my gran. These are. These are for you.

A moment.

SOPHIE shuts the drawer. She hasn't found what she was looking for.

SOPHIE. Where's that spanner, Pete?

PETE. Sorry?

SOPHIE. What have you done with that spanner?

PETE. It's just…

　　PETE *finds it in his pocket*.

SOPHIE. Nice one. Perfect.

　　SOPHIE *jumps up. She moves* PETE *to stand behind the door.*

PETE. What you doing?

SOPHIE. Just stand here.

PETE. Um.

SOPHIE. Billy!

PETE. Oh, Soph, no.

SOPHIE. Shh.

PETE. Not tonight, please.

SOPHIE. Quiet.

PETE. Have you not had enough today?

SOPHIE. Exactly.

PETE. What d'you mean?

SOPHIE. Now's the perfect time, when he's not…

　　Billy!

PETE. I'm really not sure tonight's –

SOPHIE. Don't be a twat, Pete.

PETE. Meant to be getting my gran's prescription.

SOPHIE. Shut up. Get ready.

　　Billy, will you get your arse down here please!

BILLY (*off*). Just a sec.

SOPHIE. No, Billy. Now!

PETE. Well I'm not using this.

SOPHIE. He's got to learn.

PETE. I know but.

SOPHIE. They'll have bloody, knives and that. Crowbars.

PETE. I'll hurt him though.

SOPHIE. If he's listened, you won't.

PETE. Right.

No. Can't do it. I just, I can't.

SOPHIE. No point faffing about, Pete.

PETE. I'm putting it down.

He puts the spanner down. SOPHIE *sighs.*

What?

SOPHIE. Such a wuss.

PETE. I'm doing my best, Soph. It's quite short notice.

PETE *starts jiggling up and down on the spot a bit, limbering up.*

SOPHIE. Billy!

BILLY (*off*). What's the matter?

SOPHIE. Never mind what's the matter, just bloody.

You ready?

PETE *nods.*

Do it properly? Like I showed you just.

SOPHIE *mimes a grab.* PETE *nods.*

Right, he's…

PETE. Okay, okay.

BILLY *comes in.*

BILLY. What's up? What's –

PETE *runs out from behind the door, shouts and attacks him. Very gently. He ends up sort of hugging him from behind.*

Um. Is something…?

PETE *lets go.* SOPHIE *looks cross.*

SOPHIE. Well, that was shit.

PETE. Sorry.

SOPHIE. Both of you.

BILLY. I'm still not…

PETE. Didn't want to hurt him.

SOPHIE. Just cuddle him, is that it?

PETE. Should've done it yourself then.

SOPHIE. I needed to watch.

BILLY. I'm sorry but.

SOPHIE. How many times have we done this, Billy? How
    many times have I told you, talked you through, shown you
    what to do in this scenario?

BILLY. What you on about?

SOPHIE. Billy.

It dawns on BILLY.

BILLY. Oh, shit. Sorry.

    I just, I wasn't expecting it.

SOPHIE. That's fucking. That's the point.

BILLY. In the kitchen though.

SOPHIE. It could happen in your kitchen. There'll be knives.

PETE. Or spanners.

    BILLY *smiles*.

SOPHIE. It's not funny, Billly.

BILLY. I know but, you know. I'm a wimp really, not a…
    Someone tries to attack me, I'll just run away.

SOPHIE. Doesn't work like that.

    BILLY *sighs, rolls his eyes*.

BILLY (*to himself*). Fuck's sake.

SOPHIE. Just want you to be safe.

BILLY. And I just want everyone to stop bloody, sticking their oar in flipping, interfering. It's, you know, hard enough to be, go off on your own and, enough to think about without you lot doom-mongering all the time. Went down for the interview, never got murdered. Worst thing that happened: I got on the Circle Line in the wrong direction. But I sat it out. I just, I sat it out. So I don't see why you're suddenly getting bloody, hysterical about all, you know. I know you're just, you're trying to, but: has it ever occurred to you that maybe, maybe I'm, I'm actually a grown-up human being who's bloody, capable of looking after myself?

A moment.

SOPHIE. No that has never occurred to me.

BILLY. Whatever.

SOPHIE. I'm not being funny, Billy, last week you fell over a leaf. Yesterday you cut your thumb on a duvet.

PETE *tries not to laugh.*

BILLY. I'm not finding this useful.

SOPHIE. Again, Billy. We're doing it again.

BILLY *sighs.*

BILLY. Fine.

He leaves.

SOPHIE. Pete?

PETE *goes to wait behind the door.*

BILLY (*off*). Pete's bigger.

SOPHIE. Doesn't matter. It's balance. Turning Pete's force against him.

BILLY (*off*). The website said there's grappling.

SOPHIE. Don't mock it, Billy.

BILLY (*off*). Sorry. Sorry. Right.

BILLY *enters.* PETE *attacks.* BILLY *manages to get out of it. Ish.*

SOPHIE. Better.

BILLY. Cheers.

SOPHIE. Both of you.

BILLY. Am I done then?

SOPHIE. No, Billy, we're only just –

BILLY *sighs*.

What?

BILLY *walks away*.

BILLY. Later maybe.

SOPHIE. Billy, get back here.

BILLY. No, Soph. No.

Look, I get you're angry and that but. You've had a bad day
and that but, you know. If you want to teach someone, teach
your little girls.

Not my fault you lost it. Take it out on them.

SOPHIE. Billy.

But he's gone.

He doesn't think it's important. Fucks me off actually, cos
he'll be mixing with all these people and, he's clueless really.
Just cos they've got a sketch pad doesn't mean they're not…

PETE *doesn't know what to say*.

You should get your gran her pills.

PETE. It's alright. Open late on a Thursday so.

SOPHIE. Pete.

PETE *doesn't want to leave*.

PETE. I'll get them tomorrow.

SOPHIE. Pete, it's fine.

A moment.

PETE *goes to the door*.

PETE. I'm sorry your day's been shit.

SOPHIE *nods*.

He goes.

A moment.

He's definitely gone.

SOPHIE *picks up the flowers.*

She looks at them. Very gently smells them.

A moment.

Puts them in the bin.

6

Early morning. KATH *has got up to make some breakfast for* MARTIN *and* SOPHIE. MARTIN *is cheerily eating toast.* SOPHIE *is bleary-eyed and grumpy.* KATH *hands her a cup of black coffee. She nurses it.*

MARTIN. We'll set off when the sun gets through that spatula.

SOPHIE *is silent. She sips her coffee.*

This one's you I think.

MARTIN *hands* SOPHIE *a white coat. She doesn't put it on.*

Is it?

SOPHIE *puts it on.*

How are you getting on?

SOPHIE *sighs and shrugs. Shows him the contents of her mug.* MARTIN *smiles.*

Lovely morning.

Wonder if we'll see that woman again. On the prom. She's got a, what's-it-called bloody, labradoodle. Kath.

She wears these hats. Peruvian. Stupid great grin on her face.

Silence.

Things like that.

I remember when we first started, been doing it about a
month, hadn't we, Kath? And we were sick of it really.

KATH. I was.

MARTIN. Mornings and, miserable. And this tiny old lady, one
of the bungalows up Seathorne started leaving jars out with
her empties. Full jars, jam and. Branston. With little notes:
'please open'.

That's when I thought, this is for me. Not just about the milk
really.

She's dead now.

KATH. She's been dead twenty years, Martin.

MARTIN. No.

KATH. She has.

MARTIN *thinks about this*.

MARTIN. You're right.

Think time does funny things to a milkman.

KATH. Does funny things to everyone.

MARTIN. No, love, think about it: you get up at the same time,
go along exactly the same roads every morning, for twenty-
odd years and, nothing changes. But also, everything
changes. Everything that's happened in all that time's just
sort of bustling round on the way. Carr's Meadow,
Beaconsfield, Chellsway, Hull Road, past the lighthouse,
Lascelles Avenue, U-turn, Arthur Street, North Road,
Waxholme Road, U-turn, Seathorne, North Prom, wave at
the sea, Bannister Street, Queen Street, Park Avenue,
Kirkfield Road, Victoria Avenue, South Cliff Road, Nutri-
Grain bar, King Street, Louville Avenue, South Prom, home.

Bet you can do that, Soph an' all.

SOPHIE *nods. She doesn't seem thrilled.*

But there's, you know. I look at grannies now, think: you
look young. Think about it some more, realise I knew their
mums. Some of them I knew their grans. PC Barker – first
morning he managed to wee in his potty, brought it out to
show me. Dead proud. See him buzzing about with his siren

now and I think: you've done alright. Not such a promising start but. Nice shops turn to pound shops. Pound shops turn to nice shops. Kids gone off to college, prison, kids gone off to bloody, Afghanistan. Kids who stick around, make more kids. More kids who want more milk.

Eh, Soph?

SOPHIE *smiles, bravely.*

Caravan site's filling up. Did you see in the *Gazette*? Withernsea: the new Skegness.

KATH. Sure you won't have something to eat, Soph?

SOPHIE. Positive.

KATH. Take these for your pocket then.

KATH *gives her two Nutri-Grain bars. She puts them in her pockets. Smiles.*

You don't have to go if you don't...

SOPHIE. It's fine.

KATH. Rough day yesterday. Your dad'll manage.

SOPHIE. It's fine.

MARTIN *looks at* SOPHIE, *encouraging.*

MARTIN. Tell her then.

KATH. Tell me what? What's up?

SOPHIE *takes a deep breath.*

SOPHIE. Me and Dad were talking and, I'm going to try and get a bit more. Learn a bit more about how to run, sort of, how to do all the books and the orders and that. Be more useful. Put more in. Get more out.

KATH. Why?

SOPHIE. Cos ju-jitsu isn't going to work.

KATH. Don't say that, Soph.

SOPHIE. Well, it isn't so.

KATH. Why not?

SOPHIE. Cos I've given up.

A moment.

KATH. What?

SOPHIE. Realised, I'm doing all this stuff, putting all this work in and it's actually, it's not helping. Getting in the way of just. It's doing my head in.

KATH. What about your girls?

SOPHIE. Sensei Steve'll take over for a couple of weeks and then, just, phase it out.

KATH. But they love it.

SOPHIE. Go to Sensei Steve's classes then.

KATH. It's different, Soph. They love you.

SOPHIE. Mum.

KATH. Hear them talking about it at school. Sensei Soph this, Sensei Soph that.

SOPHIE. Not meant to call me that.

KATH. They can't it help it, love. Kids who I never thought, little messy sorry kids, you know, lost causes really they're, they're confident they're, you know. Calm, respectful. It's worth sticking it out, Soph.

I thought after Woolies shut you were done for, no jobs left round here but I think now it was a blessing. Doing so well. And it's so you, Soph.

SOPHIE. Don't, Mum.

KATH. Feel different next week.

SOPHIE. I won't. And I don't want persuading or, I don't want to talk about it. I'm just: I'm done.

A moment.

MARTIN. Shall we…?

KATH. You're letting her give up on something this –

MARTIN. I'm being supportive, Kath. Always on at me, be more supportive. So I am.

KATH *laughs.*

KATH. Only cos it suits you.

MARTIN. We'll talk about it later.

KATH. We won't though will we? You'll scurry out the door promising, we'll somehow never quite get round to talking about it.

SOPHIE *drains her coffee*.

SOPHIE. Ready?

SOPHIE *and* MARTIN *leave*.

7

The kitchen is empty. Smoke is coming from the oven. The smoke alarm starts to beep. Eventually BILLY *appears in his pyjamas*.

BILLY. Oh, um. Argh.

BILLY *wafts the smoke ineffectively. He opens the oven door. It makes matters worse*.

Oh no. Erm…

He picks up a tea towel and tries to shoo the smoke away.

Go back go back go back.

He turns the oven off, takes the burnt cakes out. They are hotter than he's expecting and he drops them on the side quickly. They sit there, blackened and smoking. He closes the oven door and opens a window. The smoke alarm is still going strong. He gets a stool and turns it off. He moves the stool back. It starts again. He gets the stool, turns it off again. The smoke clears a bit. BILLY *gets up on the stool and takes the batteries out.* KATH *arrives from outside. She is in her lollipop-lady uniform, carrying the lollipop*.

KATH. Oh God, Billy, what's…?

BILLY. Um…

BILLY *gestures towards the cakes.*

Cakes are done.

KATH. Shit. Shit shit shit shit shit.

BILLY. Never mind.

KATH. Oh, Billy, they're ruined.

BILLY. Be alright. Bit of icing, no one'll know.

KATH. Didn't think I'd be this long but. End of term,
everything takes a bit longer.

BILLY. Not cakes.

KATH *laughs. She picks up a cake and taps it on the side. It
is solid.*

Better put this back. Just in case.

BILLY *gets the stool and puts the battery back into the smoke
alarm. He waits a moment to see if it goes off. It doesn't.*

KATH. I'll do you some more.

BILLY. Pardon?

KATH. To take with you. Wouldn't've done them now but
they're better if you give them a few weeks to sort of. Before
you. Your dad said he won't want to be dragging fruitcakes
with him to London but I thought, better to have something
home-made.

BILLY. Mm.

They ponder the cakes.

Hope it's not a sign. D'you think it is?

Mum?

KATH. What's up, love?

BILLY. D'you think it's a sign? The cakes?

KATH. It's a sign I'm losing it. Never mind. Make some more
this afternoon.

BILLY. You don't have to, Mum.

KATH. No trouble, a few fruitcakes.

BILLY. That's not what I –

KATH. Keep your strength up, all that drawing. Hope seven's enough.

BILLY. Thing is though, Mum, I've been thinking about all this, all this going to college and everything and, you know, I wonder if it'd be better to just, sort of: not.

KATH. Not what?

BILLY. Um. Not go?

KATH. What?

BILLY. Wonder if I'd be better off just staying here. With you and Dad and everything. Soph.

KATH. Billy, you were desperate to get in.

BILLY. And I did get in. So I sort of think: job done.

KATH. What? What's brought this on?

BILLY. Nothing.

KATH. Well, something must've –

BILLY. I don't know. I dunno.

KATH. You must do.

> BILLY *shrugs*.

> Tell me then.

> *Silence*.

> If you don't tell me I can't help.

BILLY. Can't help anyway, can you?

KATH. Try me.

> BILLY *sighs*.

BILLY. Fine. Keep thinking about this.

> BILLY *takes the letter offering him a place at college out of his pocket. It is well-thumbed.*

> I mean, what're they on about: 'kitsch'?

KATH. What is? Dolly Parton?

BILLY *nods*.

BILLY. It's heartfelt. Not flipping, kitsch. I painted a picture of someone I love. That's it.

KATH. You put the sequins on.

BILLY. But I mean, they think I'm something I'm not don't they? Cleverer or, cooler or something. And that's just... Honestly, Mum, at the interview, all these, these proper arty people with sort of the, the hair and. I know already, I won't fit in. Ripped jeans. Everywhere you look: ripped jeans. Well, I'm sorry but, I'm not wearing ripped jeans. For anyone. Life's draughty enough.

KATH *smiles*.

KATH. Get you some long johns.

BILLY. That's not what I meant.

KATH. Well, you can't not go, Billy.

BILLY *looks sad*.

What would you do instead? Eh? (*Laughing*.) Help your dad?

BILLY *doesn't say anything*.

You're kidding me.

BILLY. I don't know.

KATH. No. No. I can't have three of you –

BILLY. What?

KATH. I'm sorry, Billy, the milk round's not an option.

BILLY. It is for Soph.

KATH. It is at the moment. And she's hardly enjoying it. Besides which, she's quite... I don't think you're really milkman material.

BILLY. Cheers, Mum.

KATH. Come on, Billy, I know you try but. Most of the stuff you do for your dad could be done just as well by a traffic cone. Better, probably. Propping gates open. Stopping people parking him in. You're much better sticking to your art and that.

BILLY. They'll all be from proper, you know, proper good places. Kent.

KATH. Billy.

BILLY. They will.

KATH. Listen to me, Billy, just. You're as good as any of them. No, listen to me. You are. Doesn't matter about their hair or their holey jeans that they got in bloody, Kent. They picked you just the same.

BILLY. But –

KATH. You'll be with people who are on your level for once. Cos, your dad and me, we love you to bits but. We are essentially hobbits. Aren't we though? Short and, you know, unadventurous. Hairy feet. Not even sure what kitsch is. Think I've been saying it quiche.

BILLY *frowns*.

But we're fine here, me and your dad, we're happy. Settled. And Soph isn't but. She'll get there. You though. There's a bit of you that's not quite, I don't know. Nourished or...? You need culture and. Buses. I think if you're serious about – and you are, Billy, I know you are, no shrugging, surprised you don't sleep with them pastels... This is a very good place to come from. Cos it's knackered and funny and it's falling in the sea. And you look at things through that set of glasses. But it's not a good place to end up.

BILLY *thinks about this*.

You can always, always come back if it all. Don't know what you'll do – don't know what any of us'll be doing but. You know. Time for a leap, I reckon.

AUTUMN

8

PETE *is laid on the kitchen floor, wearing a head torch, exploring under the sink.* SOPHIE *enters.* PETE *sits up, excited. He is dying to tell her something.*

SOPHIE. Let me guess: blockage located.

PETE. Did you see it? When you came in?

SOPHIE. What?

PETE. Oh no, you've got to... Go look, go and look.

SOPHIE. Look at what?

PETE. My van! My flipping, my new van. New to me.

SOPHIE *goes to the door and looks out.*

A moment.

SOPHIE. Pete, your new van is pink.

PETE. I know, it's amazing. I'm going to put my name on the side, and the number and everything, I thought maybe I'd put 'no job too big or small' and everyone'll remember it, cos it's, you know: eye-catching isn't it? It's, um. It's pink.

SOPHIE. Very pink.

PETE. Shocking.

SOPHIE. That is a very pink van.

PETE. Do you love it?

SOPHIE *looks nonplussed. Shrugs.*

SOPHIE. Yeah.

PETE. D'you want to come for a drive in it?

SOPHIE. No.

PETE. I've finished down here, got the new bits in. The ones that are. So we can –

SOPHIE. Just about cope with the moped, Pete. Draw the line at…

PETE. Oh.

SOPHIE *relents*.

SOPHIE. I'm kidding, it looks. You know. Roomy.

PETE. It is roomy. It is.

SOPHIE. And you're obviously thrilled.

PETE. Yep. Cheers.

SOPHIE. So that's. Good.

PETE. Mm.

A moment.

D'you want to then? Come for a drive.

SOPHIE. To be honest, Pete, I'm knackered.

PETE. I thought we could go up –

SOPHIE. No.

Pause.

PETE. You alright, Soph?

SOPHIE. I'm fine.

PETE. Seem a bit…

SOPHIE. I'm fine just. Been lugging empties round all afternoon. It's not my thing.

A moment.

PETE. What is your thing, Soph?

SOPHIE. Don't start.

PETE. I'm just saying, been helping your dad for ages now, and it's not exactly growing on you. And I really like your dad and everything but, he just seems to put on you more and more –

SOPHIE. We're busy.

PETE. Thought you were losing customers.

SOPHIE. We are.

PETE. How come you're busy then?

SOPHIE. Dunno just. Something's up with the float, makes this noise when it starts like – (*Makes the noise.*) Dad's trying to work out what's up so. I'm in charge of, sort of: other stuff.

A moment.

Just cos I'm not doing cartwheels at your frigging pink van, Pete –

PETE. It's not the van, Soph, it's. I mean, it does mean a lot to me, to have a van and everything. Cos I'm all, you know, now. I'm my own... And you're right probably, a white van, or a blue van might've been better but I'll be honest, I don't have a lot put by at the moment. Not sure how much you know about the used-van market, I've only recently been introduced to it myself but, turns out: second-hand vans, third-hand vans even, they're still quite expensive. Whereas second- or third- or, you know, fourth-hand vans that are also pink – slightly cheaper. So: no, it's not perfect. It is a very pink van. But I just want to be a plumber, and I'm doing it. I'm actually doing it. Found something I love doing.

SOPHIE. It's not that good, Pete.

PETE. Just want you to be happy, Soph.

SOPHIE. Can we talk about something else please?

A moment. PETE *shrugs.*

PETE. If you like.

SOPHIE. How's your gran doing?

PETE *nods.*

PETE. Alright I think. She's, yeah. She's, you know.

She's getting quite into hip hop.

SOPHIE. What?

PETE. Think Billy must've shown her how YouTube works when he made that video, now she's. I mean it started with Justin Timberlake and that but it's a slippery slope isn't it? Her favourite's Jay-Z. I imagine he's thrilled.

SOPHIE. So she just…?

PETE. Can't really do much now after the… Gets really out of breath so, yeah. Spends a lot of time, you know. Sitting and that. Likes my laptop cos it keeps her legs warm.

SOPHIE. But she's alright.

PETE. Yeah. Ish. Doctor said it was her heart so. Got some pills. Think it's just old age though really.

SOPHIE. Poor Edna.

PETE. Eighty-three years. Lot of heartbeats.

SOPHIE. Must feel a bit…

PETE. What?

SOPHIE. Dunno. Must miss doing stuff. Feel a bit empty and that.

I would.

PETE *sighs*.

PETE. Is this about ju-jitsu?

SOPHIE. What?

PETE. Cos you can just go back.

SOPHIE. It's not about ju-jitsu.

PETE. I think it is about ju-jitsu though.

SOPHIE. Well, it's not about ju-jitsu.

PETE. You can start again.

SOPHIE. Not that simple.

PETE. It is though.

SOPHIE. Pete. Leave it.

PETE. Sorry.

A moment.

No, actually.

SOPHIE. What?

PETE. If it's alright I'll just plough on, put my foot in it.

SOPHIE *smiles*.

SOPHIE. If you must.

PETE. I just think, you're really good at stuff. You should be doing something you love. Or, you know. Like at least. And what you like is: ju-jitsu. And you got so close. Why not just go back, get your black belt and then, you know. The world's your oyster really. Ju-jitsu-wise.

SOPHIE. Cos I don't want to.

PETE. You do though.

SOPHIE. I don't. I don't have it in me.

PETE. I think the opposite is true. I mean: that examiner. You bloody. You showed him.

SOPHIE *sighs*.

SOPHIE. No I didn't, Pete.

PETE. You did though.

SOPHIE. I didn't.

Meant to be defensive isn't it – ju-jitsu? Peaceful. You're meant to use your opponent's force against them. Leverage or. Not attack. And you're certainly not meant to use it to sort of, get things off your chest. Like, you shouldn't, I dunno. If you're frustrated or angry or something, you shouldn't. Only use force in self-defence. Or defending someone else. Not cos a dickhead calls you feisty. He did it to rile me and, you know, shouldn't've let it get to me but.

PETE. Oh, Soph. Loads of things don't work out first time.

SOPHIE. That's not what I'm saying.

PETE. I took seven driving tests.

SOPHIE. Yeah. You're a shit driver.

A moment.

PETE. Do you remember what you told me after…?

SOPHIE *looks confused.*

You must do.

SOPHIE. After what?

PETE. Just got our marching orders from Woolies, on the way out, cramming our pockets full of pick 'n' mix. Said I must be glad of the free time, cos it meant I could take my love of drains to the next level. Kidding I think but, you know. It was actually true. I asked you what you'd do now and you just… this plan just came out all sort of, ready. Said you'd help your dad out to get by till you got your black belt. And then you'd teach self-defence classes for women in nearby village halls. Been meaning to do it for ages but you needed a bit of a push. Do you not…?

SOPHIE *doesn't answer.*

And honestly, Soph, it just, blew me away. That's when I knew, you know. When I first sort of… If I had to pick a moment. Just thought it sounded…

Borrow my moped if that'd help. It's only sitting there.

SOPHIE *is silently crying.*

You alright? Soph?

No answer.

Oh God, Soph, didn't mean to –

SOPHIE. I'm fine.

PETE *tries to comfort her. A hand on her shoulder. She shakes it off.*

I'm fine, Pete, don't…

PETE. I've upset you though.

SOPHIE. I'm. Fine.

PETE. You don't have to do this, Soph.

SOPHIE. What?

PETE. You do this thing, do this thing where, give me this little glimpse of, I dunno, just see a little bit of you. And I can see something's up, Soph, something's really. And I'm trying to be a good, try to be a good, you know. But you don't give much back, Soph. Do you though? Don't give me any sort of. Just. Always just, shoving me away.

SOPHIE. Take the hint then, Pete.

PETE. What?

SOPHIE. Fuck off.

PETE. But –

SOPHIE. Do you think I haven't have noticed, Pete? That my life is shit? D'you think I need to hear it from a fucking, plumber?

PETE. Soph, that isn't what –

SOPHIE. Fuck off, Pete!

PETE. Soph.

SOPHIE. Fuck off!

SOPHIE *gathers up* PETE*'s tools. Shoves them at him. He picks them up, distraught. Leaves.*

9

MARTIN *is sitting at the kitchen table, head in hands.* KATH *enters, in dinner-lady overalls, drenched.*

KATH. I got playground duty. They call this drizzle.

MARTIN *smiles.*

Off for a shower.

MARTIN. Soph's in, I think. We had the same.

KATH *thinks.*

KATH. I'll just stand here and drip.

KATH *puts down two bits of newspaper – one to stand on, one to put her wet clothes on, as she undresses. She gets down to her undies.*

MARTIN. Is this necessary? In the kitchen.

KATH (*smiles*). Little treat.

MARTIN*'s not so sure.*

It is really. This pig lorry went past when I was walking home, think he did it on purpose, through this huge puddle full of. Dread to think. And a bit of, liquid sort of sloshed out the back an' all. Of the lorry. So. I'm drenched and I hum. Don't want it traipsing round the house.

KATH *looks down at her washed-out grey-looking bra and big pants. A bit wistful.*

I used to be a sex kitten.

MARTIN. Wish you'd told me.

They smile.

KATH. Sod off.

Wouldn't've noticed anyway.

MARTIN. I would've.

KATH. When?

MARTIN. When I was younger. My youth.

KATH. You never had a youth, Martin. You had a milk round.

MARTIN *looks downcast.* KATH *bundles the clothes up and goes out. Comes back in again in a coat. Opens it.*

Look I'm a flasher.

They laugh.

MARTIN. In thermal pants.

KATH. I'm one of them exhibitionists.

MARTIN. You're a nutter.

KATH. I know it's my age.

MARTIN. D'you think?

KATH. Honestly, you've got years of this.

MARTIN. Can't wait.

> MARTIN *stands up and hugs her. It is very loving. He holds her for a long time. Puts his head on her shoulder.*

KATH. You alright, love?

> *He kisses her head.*

> Martin?

> MARTIN *sighs.*

MARTIN. Not quite.

KATH. Is it your shoulder?

> MARTIN *smiles.*

> I can give it a rub.

MARTIN. It's not my shoulder.

KATH. Thought it helped the other night.

MARTIN. Kath.

KATH. I'll be gentle. Gentler.

MARTIN. Not my shoulder, love. It's my milk float.

> *They separate.*

KATH. Oh.

> What's happened with your milk float?

MARTIN. I don't know really. Just: died. Louville Avenue. Had to tow it home.

KATH. You can fix it though?

> MARTIN *shakes his head.*

> Take it to the garage then, don't sit here worrying about it.

MARTIN. They said it's not.

KATH. What?

MARTIN. Said it'll cost more to mend than it's worth so…

A moment.

KATH. What'll you do?

MARTIN. Well, this is the thing really. I need a new one.

KATH. Do you?

MARTIN. Not new new. New to me.

KATH. How much is that going to cost?

MARTIN. Doesn't matter, love, we need one don't we?

KATH. Do we?

MARTIN. Course we do. Can't do it on foot, can I? Can't do it in the Corsa.

KATH. You could at a push. Few trips.

MARTIN. I'd be a laughing stock. And Soph.

KATH. But it'd do the job though. For a bit.

A moment.

MARTIN *looks sad.*

MARTIN. You think we shouldn't replace it.

KATH. I didn't say that.

MARTIN. You've got to spend money to make money. That's the rules.

KATH. You've got to spend money wisely.

MARTIN. It's a business, Kath.

KATH. It's only a business if it makes a profit. At the moment it's a hobby. A habit.

MARTIN. I don't think that's true, Kath.

KATH. It is, love. It is. And Soph'd be better off signing on. That's just, that's definitely… I'm not saying this to upset you, I'm saying this to try and get through to you. Said the summer would sort you out. It hasn't. You're worse off than

ever, customers cancelling left right and centre and still
you're wanting to… The truth is: it's. Nobody needs a
milkman any more. Do they though? Handful of people. The
world's moved on. Even, you know. Here.

Selling hummus now, in Tesco.

MARTIN *contemplates this*.

Tastes like grout.

MARTIN. So I'm useless then. Is that what…?

KATH. No.

MARTIN. Fighting a losing battle.

KATH *thinks. Nods*.

KATH. Maybe. I don't know. What do you think?

MARTIN. I think it's. I think you can't have a milk round
without a float.

KATH. Well then: your decision.

10

KATH, SOPHIE *and* MARTIN *are in the kitchen. The milk float
is about to be towed away for scrap.* KATH *is watching through
the window.* MARTIN *is sitting down.* SOPHIE *is leaning
against the sink, watching them both.*

KATH. You're sure about this, Martin?

MARTIN *doesn't say anything*.

Cos he's not left yet. You can still change your mind, if it
doesn't feel right. He's eating a sandwich.

MARTIN. I just want him to go.

KATH. You heard what he said though, it's not too late. Said
he's had a few like this and they're not as expensive as you
think. To repair them.

So I'm sure you could change your mind if...

SOPHIE *doesn't know what to do*.

You wouldn't be the first, Martin, I reckon.

MARTIN. I've told everyone now. It's done.

SOPHIE. Were they upset?

MARTIN *shakes his head*.

MARTIN. Relieved, I think. Not a big change really. For them.

KATH. But you have to be sure.

MARTIN. It's going. That's that. Worth more for scrap than...

MARTIN *shows* KATH *a roll of notes*.

He'll finish his sandwich and go.

A moment.

KATH. Feels like I've rushed you into it.

KATH *gets a bit choked up*.

It's nothing, you know. To unload it. Get it patched up. Only money. We'd manage, wouldn't we, Soph?

SOPHIE *doesn't say anything*.

You could have my 20ps.

MARTIN. What's he messing about at?

SOPHIE. Big sandwich.

MARTIN. Bloody hell.

SOPHIE. Think it's a baguette.

Silence.

Wish Billy was here. He'd. You know.

MARTIN. Put his CD on, eh? Bit of thingy, Dolly. Calm your mum down a bit.

SOPHIE *gets on with this*.

KATH. I'm sorry, Martin, it's… Feel like I've…

MARTIN. Sshh, love. Come sit here.

There's, you know. Soph can get back to her… I'll sort something for.

Come sit by me, eh? Sit by me.

KATH *sits by* MARTIN. *Dolly Parton's 'I Will Always Love You' starts to play.*

There we go. Lovely one this.

KATH. Favourite.

MARTIN *puts his good arm round* KATH. *They sit and listen.* SOPHIE *mooches around in the background. By the second verse* KATH *is in tears.*

SOPHIE. Not sure this is helping.

KATH. It's the words really.

SOPHIE. It's not about a milk float.

MARTIN. No, but.

SOPHIE *doesn't know what to do. She turns the music off.*

MARTIN *and* KATH *are holding each other.* KATH *is sobbing.* MARTIN *looks devastated.*

SOPHIE *can't watch. She looks out of the window instead.*

We hear a lorry pull away.

SOPHIE. He's gone then. It's gone.

KATH *does her best to stop sobbing.*

MARTIN *nods. He takes the money he got from the scrap man and puts it in* KATH's *jar of twenty-pence pieces.*

They look at each other.

MARTIN *goes upstairs.*

11

The kitchen is empty. PETE *knocks and pops his head round the door. Nobody answers. He is wearing a black suit and tie, and carrying lots of empty dishes.*

PETE. Hello?

No answer. PETE *comes in. Puts the empty dishes on the table. He takes a little bag of weed out and puts it on the top. Thinks better of it. Puts it back in his pocket.*

Hello?

Still no answer.

PETE *goes to leave. The sink catches his eye. He tries the tap. It works perfectly. He turns it on and off again. Still fine. He bobs his head under the sink to look at the pipes he fitted.*

KATH *enters.*

KATH. Hiya, Pete.

PETE *jumps, bangs his head. Stands up.*

PETE. The door was open, sorry.

KATH *smiles.*

I was just, but. Still going strong so. Strong-ish.

KATH. You alright, love?

PETE. Oh yeah.

He rubs his head.

Happens a lot.

KATH. No, I meant.

PETE. Oh. Um.

KATH. Soph's out with her dad.

PETE. I know. I mean, not that it'd. Just didn't want to, cos we've been a bit. But anyway. Just fetching these back really. Someone's washed them, don't know who. It all got. I got a bit overtook.

KATH. Thanks, love.

PETE. No, no, thank you.

KATH. Hope it was alright.

PETE. Just right. Thank you.

KATH. Sometimes worry I go a bit far with buffets.

PETE. No it was. Perfect, Gran would've... Never seen so many bhajis.

I've got some money for, so –

KATH. Don't be daft, Pete.

PETE. I'm not, must've cost a –

KATH. Put it away, you. Just thought it'd be one less thing.

PETE. Well. Thank you.

KATH. Do you want a cup of tea?

PETE. I better not. Won't sleep otherwise. I should...

KATH. You sure you're alright?

PETE. Oh yeah, yeah.

KATH. Lovely service.

PETE *nods*.

PETE. Everyone says it's the worst bit so. Glad it's...

I mean it isn't the worst bit, the worst bit was sort of, finding her.

Or, you know the, the cemetery and that, today.

I mean she was quite jolly about it, my gran. Always said when the time comes, just pop me in on top of your granddad. Said she preferred being on top anyway, so.

But I mean, you know my. I dunno my. My mum and dad are, they're buried in Preston aren't they? Bloody, other side of the country. Used to go together, me and Gran. Now though. Just think like: fucking hell. I'm twenty-three. Got all these graves to look after. And the, the headstones get this sort of I dunno, this sort of algae, this sort of black algae on them, it's a nightmare. Got to really scrub to get it off and I just think: that's my job now isn't it? I mean I don't mind, not at all, I just. You know.

KATH. Oh, love.

She gives him an enormous hug.

Don't think about that tonight.

I'll come with you. When you're ready I'll. I'll come with you.

PETE (*quietly*). Thank you.

KATH. Don't give it another thought.

KATH *lets* PETE *go. He looks grateful. Then a bit awkward.*

PETE. Um.

KATH. What is it?

PETE. No. Doesn't matter.

KATH. Eh?

PETE. Nothing, just. It's a bit. Cos Billy told her once about all the, things you've been cooking. Something new every day and that. She was always asking what the latest was. Courgette muffins –

KATH. They weren't a success.

PETE. Anyway she, yeah, thought you might like to try, um.

PETE *gives* KATH *the weed.*

This. Don't have to. I just said I'd… Gran thought it'd be funny.

KATH. Oh, poppet.

KATH *starts to laugh.*

You keep it eh? Do you good.

PETE. I've got loads, honestly. Found loads, I mean. Think she might've been… I've had quite a few phone calls about it since.

KATH is still smiling. PETE joins in.

KATH. Well, it's a lovely thought, Pete, but. I wouldn't know where to start really.

PETE. You don't have to.

KATH. No, I mean, I'm quite up for having a go but…

PETE. Oh, um. Well, you can, you can bake with it or. I can roll you… If you like. Did it for my gran in the end so.

KATH considers.

KATH. Right. Right.

Come on then.

They sit down and PETE gets everything out of his pocket and gets on with it. KATH watches, fascinated.

A moment.

I might give Billy a shout.

PETE smiles.

Billy!

PETE carries on.

PETE. It was nice he came back and everything.

KATH. Don't be daft, Pete. He was ever so upset when he heard. Anyway, let's not…

BILLY enters.

BILLY. Oh alright, Pete? How you feeling?

Oh.

BILLY stops. KATH smiles.

KATH. We're just having a joint, Billy.

BILLY. Nah.

PETE. It's my gran's.

KATH. Thought you might like to join us.

BILLY *doesn't know what to do.*

BILLY. Um. Is this a test?

KATH *laughs.*

KATH. Come on, you.

BILLY *sits down.*

A moment.

Nobody really knows what to say.

PETE. Um. How's college then, Billy?

BILLY. Oh, you know. Alright.

PETE. Oh.

BILLY. It's pretty different to what I was hoping.

PETE. Suppose it takes a bit of getting used to.

BILLY. Not sure it's worth getting used to.

KATH. Billy.

BILLY. There's just, not much art I suppose. Everyone does loads of talking, and then they all do something tiny and sort of, a bit, you know, a bit shit, and then everyone takes it really seriously. And then I do stuff and sort of chuck everything I've got at it, like, everything I'm trying to… They just think I'm taking the piss.

But yeah. Got an exhibition thingy next week, like these performances we've done so. See how that goes down.

PETE. Hope it's alright.

KATH. Be fine, Pete. Billy's just a worrier. Don't know where he gets it from.

PETE *finishes.*

PETE. Here we are.

He gives KATH *the joint. She laughs.*

KATH. Oh dear.

PETE. Plenty left, if you…

KATH. Right. Right.

A moment.

Shall we just, do it then?

BILLY *laughs.*

Got a lighter?

PETE. Sorry.

BILLY *finds some matches in the drawer.*

I don't normally. I mean, I've never, actually.

KATH. Me neither.

PETE. What if they come back?

KATH *shrugs.*

KATH. Sod them.

BILLY. Mum.

PETE. Won't they smell it though?

KATH. Just tell Martin it's pizza. Tell him everything's pizza.

PETE. But Soph though.

KATH. Oh she won't mind.

BILLY. Might think it's a bit weird.

PETE. But I mean, we've not been, really. I've not really seen
    her, properly, for… I mean today obviously but you can't
    really talk can you? Not properly. And, like. Before
    everything with. We had a bit of a. We had words.

KATH. Oh.

PETE. Yeah. Told me to fuck off so. Thought I would really.

KATH *looks a bit concerned.*

KATH. Not to worry, love.

A moment.

Don't have the first clue what I'm…

PETE. Think you just…

She lights up. Inhales.

KATH. Crikey.

She has another drag.

Well this is. Crikey.

She offers PETE *the joint. He shakes his head. She gives it to* BILLY.

You're welcome here any time you know, Pete. Don't be miserable on your own. Just, come over and… I mean, might just end up being miserable with Martin but still. Better than…

PETE *nods.*

PETE. Maybe.

BILLY. Pete?

He offers PETE *the joint.* PETE *shakes his head.*

PETE. Better not.

KATH. I will.

KATH *takes it off* BILLY. *She's enjoying it.* PETE *isn't sure what to do.*

PETE. Is your mum alright?

BILLY *looks.*

BILLY. To be honest, Pete: think she might be a bit stoned.

A moment.

KATH. Have some of this, love.

PETE *takes it. Has a little drag. Coughs a bit.*

You'll sleep tonight.

PETE *smiles.* KATH *laughs.*

WINTER

12

Bits of holly and fairy lights are dotted about the kitchen.

MARTIN, SOPHIE, KATH *and* BILLY *are sitting at the table. Underwhelmed, in paper hats.*

MARTIN. Sushi?

KATH *nods.*

KATH. Is it a step too far?

MARTIN. On Christmas Day? Bloody... Yes. Yes it is.

KATH. Just thought it'd be...

MARTIN. Thought it'd be what? Shit?

KATH *sighs.*

KATH. Just, nice. Sort of, everyone digging in. As a family. It was this or fondue.

A moment.

MARTIN. I'm having a sandwich.

MARTIN *gets up.*

SOPHIE. Might have one too.

KATH. Billy?

KATH *offers him the sushi.*

BILLY. Just had a selection box actually. Everything but the Chomp. Not quite ready for...

KATH. It's not all fish.

BILLY. Still though.

KATH. There's little rice parcels. Wrapped in seaweed. Veggie ones too.

BILLY. Think maybe a sandwich might be –

MARTIN. You can make your own.

A moment.

BILLY. I will do, Dad.

MARTIN. Seem to be making a lot of your own decisions lately.

KATH. Martin, can you just let it rest for a bit please? Not crowbar it into the –

MARTIN. I'm not crowbarring anything.

KATH. You are, love. It didn't even make sense.

BILLY. It's the right decision, Dad.

MARTIN. Oh is it? Very good then.

SOPHIE. Dad.

MARTIN *is furiously buttering bread.*

MARTIN. No, Soph, don't. If he thinks he can just, drop out of college, leave his halls, go live in some filthy squat.

BILLY. It's a maisonette.

MARTIN. How are you paying for that then? With your job?

BILLY. Well. Yeah.

Least I've got a job.

KATH. Billy.

MARTIN. In a call centre.

BILLY. Yes.

MARTIN. And that's better than being at college is it? Getting your qualifications and –

BILLY. It is actually.

MARTIN. Never heard anything so fucking ridiculous.

BILLY. I was getting chucked out anyway.

MARTIN. Should've worked harder then. Tried a bit more.

A moment.

BILLY. I tried a lot.

KATH *touches* BILLY*'s arm.*

KATH. That's enough buttering now, Martin.

MARTIN *puts the knife down. Sighs.*

There's cheese in the fridge.

SOPHIE *passes the cheese.* MARTIN *cuts two big slabs, makes two rough sandwiches, puts one down in front of* SOPHIE *and starts to eat the other himself.*

Well, I'm having a bit anyway.

KATH *has a bit of sushi. It doesn't go down well.*

Shame Pete couldn't make it.

MARTIN. What's Pete got to do with…

KATH. Just saying, thought he might be lonely today but. Soph asked him, said he's busy.

BILLY. What's he up to?

KATH. Oh now. Where's he going?

SOPHIE*'s got a mouthful of sandwich. Says something.*

That's it.

Nobody else understood.

Danny's.

BILLY. In Tenerife?

KATH. No, love. Queen Street.

BILLY. Danny's in Tenerife though. Whole of Christmas. He got a deal, last minute.

The penny drops.

KATH. Did you actually ask Pete?

SOPHIE. Course I did.

KATH. But he said Danny's?

SOPHIE. Yes.

KATH. But Danny's in Tenerife? Definitely?

BILLY. Keeps putting photos on Facebook.

KATH. Poor Pete.

MARTIN. What d'you mean? Lucky to miss this.

KATH. He'll be sat on his own in his dead gran's house, no one to talk to, nothing. Heartbroken. Probably having something limp out the microwave.

MARTIN. Better than sushi. Least it's cooked.

SOPHIE. Maybe he just wants a bit of time on his own.

KATH. No, love.

SOPHIE. His own space.

KATH. He thinks he's upset you.

SOPHIE. What?

KATH. Thinks you're not speaking to him.

SOPHIE. Oh, frigging. I rang him up! God.

> KATH *gives* SOPHIE *a look.*

> Can't be doing with. Doing my head in.

> *A moment.*

KATH. Right then.

MARTIN. Right then what?

KATH. Sorry about this, I've decided.

> KATH *jumps up, goes in a drawer, grabs the hammer and attacks the taps. They start to spray water out.*

MARTIN. The fuck are you doing, Kath?

KATH. The time has come.

She keeps hitting the sink. Goes underneath and smacks the pipes too. Water leaks out.

MARTIN. Stop it you're –

KATH. Ring Pete. Tell him it's an emergency.

SOPHIE. Mum.

KATH. I'm not kidding. Tell him now. Come now.

SOPHIE. I don't want –

KATH. It's not about you, Sophie, any of you. It's about bloody, making a little change. Letting some tiny changes happen without the world ending. And I've been bloody, coaxing all of you out of your little ruts all bloody year, just for things to be: slightly better. Can't even do that. I've got you two sitting round miserable as sin, getting nostalgic about a milk float that wasn't any good to anyone. Billy's doing God knows what in London, haven't got a cat in hell's chance of getting my head round that. All I want, all I bloody want from the years and years of bloody, listening, supporting, feeding, washing, hugging, dropping off, picking up, hanging on to, all the work I've put into this fucking family, is for the four of us to just: manage. That is all I want.

A moment. KATH stops hammering. She looks a bit embarrassed.

MARTIN. And a new sink, presumably.

KATH (*defeated*). I don't think it's much to ask, Martin: running water.

MARTIN. Well. It's running now.

This takes KATH by surprise. She finds it funny.

A moment.

BILLY. I'll ring Pete.

BILLY goes to the phone. Water is leaking everywhere. KATH looks anxious.

KATH. Quickly, Billy, if you can.

13

PETE *is laid under the sink with his head torch.* SOPHIE *is stood in the doorway, a bit uncertain about coming in.*

PETE. You can come in, Soph, it's all. Think it's safe.

SOPHIE. Thought I might mop a bit.

She starts.

There is a bit of silence.

You alright then?

PETE *doesn't say anything.*

Must miss her.

PETE. Just try to keep busy really. You know what it's like.

SOPHIE. Yeah.

Though, I don't really, to be honest.

She's sort of the first person I've properly known who's…

PETE. Oh.

SOPHIE. You've had loads.

A moment.

PETE. It's not a competition, Soph.

SOPHIE. No. Course it isn't, shit, sorry that came out… I just meant…

PETE. I know.

A moment.

PETE *sits up. Smiles.*

It's nice talking to you, Soph.

SOPHIE *looks relieved. Smiles. She crouches down next to* PETE. *Peers under the sink.*

SOPHIE. How're you getting on?

PETE. Well, it's. It's basically fucked.

SOPHIE. Good work, Mum.

PETE. Mustn't use it any more but. Think I've stopped the leaks. Need the water back on really, to check. But if your mum's getting a new one tomorrow then, in the sales then. Yeah. Should be fine.

SOPHIE. Ace.

Pause.

Sure you're alright?

PETE *nods*.

PETE. Bit excited actually.

SOPHIE. Oh right?

PETE. Booked a plane ticket this morning. Online. My gran left me a bit of, so I just thought: yeah. Australia. Three months. Clear my head a bit.

SOPHIE. Brilliant.

PETE. Apparently you can plumb your way along the coast so. Thought I would. Come back with a nice tan.

SOPHIE *pulls a face*.

What?

SOPHIE. You don't go brown, Pete. You go pink.

PETE *shrugs*.

PETE. Least it'll match my van.

SOPHIE *smiles*.

SOPHIE. When are you off?

PETE. Third of January.

SOPHIE. Shit.

PETE. Thought, you know. Sooner the better really.

SOPHIE *nods*.

A moment.

Had a chat with Danny the other day.

SOPHIE. Did he take the piss?

PETE. Just the usual really. Love-life mockery.

SOPHIE. Have you even got a love life, Pete?

PETE. Nah. I mean, I've got a *Xena Warrior Princess* DVD and some soggy tissues but. Doesn't count apparently. Anyway though, that's not what…

Told me something about, before I came and that. Came to live.

Tell me to shut up if.

I mean tell me to fuck off.

SOPHIE. Oh.

PETE. Told me, um. Some lad at a party sort of… yeah. Tried to. Or, did he manage to? I don't know. And you had to sort of. And that's why you started ju-jitsu and that.

A moment.

I never knew that.

SOPHIE *shrugs.*

SOPHIE. Long time ago.

PETE. Yeah but, I just.

Danny said you've not really, you know, since.

So I'm sorry if I've been a bit, think I might've been a bit, pushy.

SOPHIE. Don't be daft.

PETE. And I'm sorry that bloke stopped you getting your black belt.

SOPHIE. Not your fault.

PETE. I think you'd be really good though. Good teacher. And, especially, I think you could help people be more… And you'd feel more…

A moment.

SOPHIE *(quietly).* I think you're probably right.

PETE. So. Try again?

SOPHIE. I dunno, Pete.

PETE. Talk to Sensei Steve at least.

SOPHIE shrugs.

SOPHIE. Maybe.

PETE. No, Soph. Promise.

SOPHIE sighs.

SOPHIE. Go on then.

PETE. Promise though.

SOPHIE smiles.

SOPHIE. I promise.

PETE smiles.

PETE. Right then. Sink's sorted. Said my bit. Now just: sod off to Australia.

SOPHIE. Yeah. Sod off, you.

They look at each other. Look down. Look up again.

14

Night.

MARTIN sits at the kitchen table trying to fill in an application form. He is wearing KATH's glasses.

BILLY enters.

MARTIN looks up. Glares. BILLY smiles.

BILLY. Sorry, it's the…

BILLY points to the glasses. MARTIN doesn't smile.

MARTIN. They're your mum's. Left mine somewhere.

BILLY. Suit you.

MARTIN *goes back to the form.*

What you up to?

MARTIN. Concentrating.

BILLY. What on?

MARTIN *sighs*.

MARTIN. Form.

BILLY *looks*.

BILLY. Oh.

A moment.

Don't do that tonight, Dad.

MARTIN. Got to be done.

BILLY. It's Christmas though. Day off.

MARTIN. The thing about being unemployed: days off aren't as special.

Not like working in a call centre.

BILLY. Dad.

MARTIN. What is it you do?

BILLY *looks down*.

BILLY. Put people on hold.

MARTIN *rolls his eyes*.

MARTIN. Well, anyway.

MARTIN *goes back to the form.*

BILLY. It wasn't. I didn't just sort of, on a whim or anything. I properly, properly…

MARTIN *isn't listening*.

It's like, the day after the exhibition, well, not exhibition, it was, we were doing these performances, performance art. Everyone did stuff about like genocide and that, living on council estates, even though they went to flipping, Eton or something, wear pashminas. Men in pashminas. And I was, I dunno. I'd obviously got the wrong end of the stick. Just sort of dressed up as Dolly Parton, lip-syncing to 'My Tennessee Mountain Home' in front of, did these paintings of Withernsea landmarks. The lighthouse and that. Aldi. The tutors called me in to see them the next day, sort of said: 'This isn't art, Billy, it's karaoke.' And, you know, fair enough. But then: I knew, I absolutely knew it was the best way of saying... Well, don't know what it was saying really but it was just: definitely, the best I had.

Still. Worst mark out of everyone. So, you know.

And then I came out the office, someone had bloody, stolen my paintings. Of Aldi and that.

A moment.

MARTIN. I'm sorry, Billy.

BILLY. No, it was brilliant.

MARTIN. What?

BILLY. Just spent an hour with these knobheads telling me how all my art was shit and, and worthless. But, you know. If it's worth stealing... So that was like a bit of a turning point really. For me. Thought, I can stay here getting sick of everything and, you know, miserable and that, for another three years, or, leave while I still give a shit about stuff. Sort of keep that bit of me safe. Get a crap job. Get some mates. Do some paintings, stick them up in cafés and that. Go out, dance on a table, you know, fall in love. That sort of thing happens if you... I mean it hasn't, the last lad I tried to kiss actually ducked but. It could happen. Stood there thinking: 'In this situation, what would Dolly Parton do?' So then I just sort of, yeah. Left.

MARTIN *looks bewildered.*

I've let you down haven't I?

No answer.

I have though. You think I've. Think I'm a failure.

MARTIN. I think you're an idiot.

BILLY. Well, we always knew that so…

A moment.

MARTIN. I don't think you're a failure, Billy.

BILLY *smiles*.

Cos it's actually, there's a real craft to failure. I think. Got to, got to properly work at it. Get up, put your heart into it, everything you've got into it, every day, every morning, for years and years and. Then, if you're lucky. But it's not. No guarantees. Some people put all that time in and end up bloody, doing well so.

BILLY *has stopped smiling*.

You though. Three months. Few bad marks. Not enough.

Come back in twenty-five years when you've nothing to show for it. Filling in a form for bloody, Tescos. I'll have another think then.

MARTIN *is getting a bit upset*.

BILLY. Dad.

MARTIN. It's fine, Billy.

BILLY. I'm sure there's…

Tescos doesn't work out, there's always. Pete's gran's left a gap in the. Reckon there's, there's an opportunity there.

MARTIN *smiles*.

MARTIN. Don't think your mum'd be too pleased.

BILLY. I dunno, she might surprise you.

A moment.

MARTIN *gathers himself. Clears his throat a bit. Begins again with warmth.*

MARTIN. When we started, your mum and me. Cock-up after cock-up. Didn't think we'd last five minutes. Your mum fell over everything. She'd only do it if she had a hot-water bottle with her. Thermal vest.

That was July.

BILLY. Don't blame her.

MARTIN. First winter though, this cold cold, not snowy but cold, frosty, we had this old pick-up that wouldn't start unless you left it on a slope, so we left it on the drive with all the milk and everything ready, night before. And the bastard bottles froze. Cracked. Every single...

I just thought: we're fucked. That's, you know. Hundreds of pounds, isn't it? The milk and the.

And we'd just found out your mum was pregnant with...

But she looked at me, five o'clock in the morning, grumpy as hell, with this, I don't know. Says, nobody's up, love. Won't know they were like that when we put them there. So we did. Just delivered all these broken bottles. Frozen.

Nobody said anything. Scraped through. Just about.

A moment.

But there's, you know. There's life after milk.

Hopefully.

A moment.

Hopefully.

A moment.

BILLY *moves round the table. Tentative. Hugs his dad.*

Fade.

The End.

SPACEWANG

Spacewang was first performed in a production by Hull Truck Theatre Company at Hull Truck Theatre, on 14 June 2011.

NORA   Laura Elsworthy

Director   Jane Fallowfield

NORA, *fourteen-ish.*

NORA *has a rucksack containing a shoebox covered in flashing fairy lights and home-made dials, some sparklers and a colander.*

I know it's today cos I keep picking up these signals off the spice rack. Like: 'Coriander, Coriander.' Which means 'We're on our way, seven o'clock tonight.' It is helpful, but it makes it hard to focus on your Ready brek. And I'm chewing seventy-two times for digestive reasons but with all the cosmic activity and that I just lose count.

Dad's the other side of the table staring into space. His face is all grey. Like Ready brek. He must know it's today an' all cos it's a year exactly but. Not that chatty my dad so. So it's a shit breakfast really.

And then I have to put my uniform on like I'm off to school, but it's fine, it's quite practical and hard-wearing in terms of fabric so. Stain-resistant so. Might as well.

Check one last time I've got everything with me, i.e. sandals, colander, sparklers, and I do so I just go 'Bye, Dad'. Door clicks shut. And it's only raining a bit so I just crawl into the hedge like usual. Watch everyone on their way to school. Jemma-with-a-J's there putting on lipgloss and she's singing, everyone's singing really, singing that song that's like: 'don't stop believing'. Which by the way I flipping love. But I just stay in the hedge, wait for them to leave. Cos it's, you know. It's comfy.

After a bit they all sort of shut up, sod off, and I can get out my plan of things to do for tonight. It's a three-phase plan and I'm ready really to just. I just get out the hedge, crack on.

Phase one: vodka

Shoplifting is a piece of piss. You just, you basically just: nick it. And then you get caught. And the security man goes: 'What you doing?' and you just have to say really loud: 'NO, CARL' or whatever his badge says. And if there's any old ladies nearby, or nuns and that, and there always is, they look over and Carl gets well confused. Starts steering you by your shoulders to his little office. And you hang on till you're just in the doorway then shout: 'COS I DON'T WANT TO SHOW YOU MY FANNY. AGAIN.' He panics and you just run off. Next time you nick something though he remembers what happened and you can see him thinking 'not worth it', just lets you get away with it. So you can get quite a lot of vodka really, it's no trouble. And actually I'm quite good mates with Carl now. He gives me this little nod near exotic fruit then in about five minutes he's out the back on his break. We get pissed between the wheelie bins.

And I did show him my fanny in the end but. Just to say thanks but. He wasn't fussed.

Today's a bit different though. Soon as I come in he's looking dead panicky, starts doing this, tries to sort of waft me back out the door. I just ignore it, plod on but he's in a right flap. And all this wafting? And I can see him looking at this woman. She's standing next to him with a clipboard and a little moustache, making all these notes so he doesn't know what to... Mouths something at me like: 'Go away' but, I dunno, I just mouth something back like: 'no', head for the booze. I'm umming and aahing a bit but there's signals coming off the Smirnoff so I know it's the right one. And it's buy-one-get-one-free so. Just ignore the bit about buying one. Check over my shoulder, tuck it in my pants. Quite a cold thing to tuck in your pants but. Never mind.

I can see Carl out the corner of my eye. He's getting really interested in this peanut butter. Like properly interested. Like he's getting a bit weird about the peanut butter, and the woman's thinking he's got some sort of thing about peanut butter, maybe he goes home, covers himself in peanut butter and gets local cats to lick it off. He doesn't though. Just buying me time.

And I know it's probably the last time I can do this now cos of moustache-woman and the clipboard and the peanut butter and everything. So what I do, I just, I flipping: leg it. Out the door, trollies flying, knocking over all the old ladies and the nuns and that just, flipping just: get out. On my way. And the alarm's beeping and Carl's shouting, sort of very slowly thundering after me but I'm just, I don't give a, cos, you know, today's too important. Today's too important and you need it to be just right.

You need it to be just right.

12.09 p.m.

Two hours and seventeen minutes is a long time to spend in a wheelie bin.

Too long really.

But Carl's still stomping about outside going 'Nora! Nora! You alright?' And the thing about wheelie bins: once you're in, you're in. It isn't comfy, it absolutely hums but also time's getting on. So I just set everything up on an old Tampax box like a sort of lab. Take a few readings, frequencies, coordinates and that. Just the basics.

NORA *takes the shoebox out of her bag, switches on the fairy lights, moves a few home-made dials.*

Everything seems fine. I'm still not a hundred per cent who's coming though. Apart from the obvious: i.e. you. It's either some cosmonads, and I hope it's them really because they're very friendly and I doubt they'd stick out much. Or it might be a spacewang, but they aren't as friendly. Cos they don't have their own planet. Like gypsies but. They can hover. But it's too early to tell and some of the readings are a bit unclear cos of being in a bin and everything. And also I started the vodka which doesn't always help scientifically. So I think I'll just have to wait and see. Settle back into some cardboard for a bit. And then: it starts.

Beep. Beep. Beep.

And I am like: 'shit' because actually a lot of the signals have not been as easy to hear as you might hope. This one though, this one is very clear. Loud and clear and regular. And the frequency would suggest it is very near to the bin which I wasn't expecting at all, not for another seven hours. Still loads to sort out. And I get a bit flustered because to be honest this isn't how I imagined it, seeing you again and that, just jumping out of a wheelie bin like: 'hiya'. And it's still going beep, beep, beep and I'm worried I might cry or something, I dunno, I'm cross that I'm here making a tit of myself. Should've done the other phases before the vodka. But there's nothing to to to do about it really, I'm just so glad you're here, you've come back and I'm sort of thinking 'At last!' or whatever, just, really really happy, I dunno...

And it stops.

There's this hiss.

It's the hiss a spaceship makes when the hatch opens. I can see it in my head with the ramp coming down and all the steam and lights, these big round eyes in the mist, big saucer eyes, and I just think: brilliant. Alien life forms have arrived on Earth. In Withernsea. Round the back of Aldi.

There's all these clunks and, bottles smashing. Don't know where that fits in really. And then, after a bit, I do.

It's flipping... it's the bin men.

Don't let it get to me though just. Deep breath. Pack up my stuff. Jump out the bin and leg it.

Phase two: fish and chips

The man behind the counter in The Golden Haddock is almost certainly special needs. A: he's bald but he's wearing a hair net. B: keeps making me repeat stuff.

'A table?' he goes. I nod. 'You want to book a table?'

'Yes please, table for two, seven o'clock.'

'But,' he looks round, 'it's a chip shop.'

It's as if he's only just noticed. And I could be like 'exactly', explain to him fish and chips are your favourite and that, but I actually can't be bothered, might as well be talking to a spacewang. He carries on anyway.

'I mean, we don't have any tables.'

'Where do people sit then?'

He thinks for a bit.

'They don't.'

I am getting quite exasperated. He can tell.

'They sometimes sort of lean on the window ledge. Don't know if that's...'

And it isn't really but I just think, you won't mind, it'll have to do.

'I'll reserve that for seven o'clock then. The window ledge. Mega.' And I don't give him chance to say no, just leave. So I'm feeling pretty flipping pleased with how it's all going to be honest. It is going to be one heck of a welcome back.

Then I feel a hand on my shoulder, heavy hand and I'm just like: 'shit'.

*

The kiddie-catcher is Hitler in a floral dress. Her job is catching kiddies who are twagging but she doesn't stop there, i.e. I'm fairly sure she's a cannibal. You probably don't believe me, the police didn't but, think about it: if the kids are skiving off, no one misses them. And she's looking at me with these big, hungry eyes like I'm covered in ketchup or something. Peanut butter. And it's possible – I have spent most of the morning in a wheelie bin – but still.

Licks her lips, goes: 'Coming with me then, Nora?'

But the thing about me is: I am never, ever going back to school. Promised myself after what happened in RE and that, when we were colouring in Hindu gods and and and everything had just happened with you, and the sandals and, just like a month before. So I hadn't got used to being pissed all the time. Things were a bit unpredictable and I wasn't being careful with chewing for digestive reasons. Hadn't learnt yet. Just sat there

with a load of crayons and glitter-glue and Jemma-with-a-J
starts looking round, sniffing and that, she's all: 'Nora, you
stink of shit.' And I just have to shrug and go: 'Yeah, cos I've
shat myself.' Put Vishnu in my bag. Walk out.

So that's sort of in the back of my mind when she says:
'Coming with me then, Nora?'

But also, I can't think how to get out of it. There's Carl, who to
be fair is looking quite sheepish, moustache-woman and the
kiddie-catcher. Got me sort of cornered. And I should probably
put up a fight or something, I do reckon I could have them, I
had Bethany Meadows and she's flipping, massive flipping,
eight months pregnant. But then this totally weird thing
happens. I just feel, very suddenly, very calm. Think maybe it's
best to sort of: go with it. She probably won't make me into
casserole today, just get a warning. Be over before you get here.
I mean it should be. Seven o'clock. And as long as I'm there to
welcome you, it'll be fine won't it? Be just right.

So I take a deep breath. And I just go back to school.

2.32 p.m.

It is called isolation but it's really just a room. Just a room and a
light and a desk and a bin and just, you can feel it in the air just,
loads of defeat. And I don't know what's happening, the police
might turn up or I might have to start lessons again which I
have to say would not be ideal at this point. I have to say it
would get in the way of my research a bit. Because I am
actually one of very few people who can both receive and
interpret alien signals with any proficiency. And most of them
live in America, whereas I live on Queen Street.

It's an intergalactic hub.

And it's a bit weird – thought I'd be getting bollocked but the
kiddie-catcher's being well nice. She's all: 'are you comfy' and
'call me Helen' and that. And I know she's trying to get me into
her oven, but at the same time, it's sort of alright. Says do I
want anything from the vending machine and I mean to say no
but then I just think flipping, yes. Please. I'd love a Wispa. And
she seems quite happy and that to go get it. Says she trusts me

to stay while she goes which I personally think is mental but then I'm still sitting here so it's worked.

And I'm sort of, it sounds daft considering but I'm sort of thinking: maybe school isn't that bad. Maybe, once you're back, the research and stuff won't matter so much anyway, maybe it wouldn't hurt to get some certificates, i.e. GCSE dance.

I flipping love dance.

And I'm just imagining what it'd be like to be doing some dance moves and stuff, with all the other people doing dance moves in matching leotards, laughing and, yeah, just having a laugh. And maybe if I was just, if everyone looked at me and the music got a bit louder and then, out of nowhere, I just invented a completely new kind of shimmy… Be mega, actually.

So I'm just thinking about that when I hear someone go: (*Whisper.*) 'Nora.'

And I freeze.

'Nora.'

Somebody's definitely saying 'Nora.'

NORA *gets a colander out of the rucksack.*

And this is like first, actual intergalactic contact, it's flipping, important, need to cut out all the white noise and interference and that. Focus. So I root around in my bag and find my, to put on, find my, well I mean it's technically a colander, but it's also got a lot of more scientific properties. To do with waves. And the voice goes: 'Nora, what you doing?'

And I don't know what to say really, panicking a bit, in case it's like the king of the cosmonads or something, so I just: 'I'm listening, your majesty.'

The voice starts to laugh. It's flipping, Carl. Turn round, he's at the window.

'Carl you knob, what you doing?'

He grins this massive…

'I'm rescuing you.'

And he's, you know, he's got some stepladders, got on the roof of the computer lab, got the window open enough for me to squeeze out. Clock says gone three. And the kiddie-catcher's been gone a while. Shouldn't take that long to get a Wispa. Might be doing anything, fetching police, preheating the oven. Decide it's probably worth slightly adjusting the original plan. So I do.

Phase two and a half: legging it

The trouble with Carl running away from his job and sort of kidnapping me and that is we need somewhere good to hide. But we're dead lucky really cos we're just running and laughing and that down Bannister Street, all of a sudden the church is just: there. Open. I mean it's locked and everything, but they've left a window open in the porch bit. Carl pops me through, I let him in.

It's dead quiet.

Try messing about with the organ and that, dressing up as albino monks but, sort of can't help calming down in church. Cos it's full of God really. Goddy stuff. Go upstairs to the balcony thing, lay down on the pews with kneelers for pillows. Carl gets the Smirnoff out. We down it. And he starts saying how he's not fussed about his job anyway, he was only doing it to pay off all the bills from when he had to get his stomach pumped in Magaluf and he'd lost that form you need. And he might not have to pay them anyway now cos they did find the form in the end. Cos he'd eaten it.

We're feeling a bit woozy and tired, and it's getting dark but we can't turn the lights on cos, technically, we're not meant to be here. And we've run out of things to talk about but it's only half five, bit soon to go down the beach for phase three. So what we do is: we have a little nap. I do anyway. So I don't hear him come in. But after a bit, Carl's shaking my shoulder, ever so gently. Goes like: 'sshh'. Points down the front of the church.

And it's my dad.

He's lit a candle on the little stand. Sort of kneeling down, saying some prayers and that. Having a little cry.

And I don't know what to do really. I don't know what to do.

*

How I remember you best is sticking all the stars on my
bedroom ceiling. The glow-in-the-dark ones. And explaining
about all space and galaxies, all the things you flipping love
from watching informative documentaries on BBC 2.

It's just before everything with your sandals and that.

Fun really: me and you. We're having a laugh. Some of the
constellations are made-up ones, i.e. the baguettes, the dented
bonnet, Dolly Parton. But you're finding them funny. You say
'Sometimes, Nora, it's good to think outside the box.' So when
they found your sandals on the beach that morning, just dead
neat and everything, on the tideline, and everyone was saying,
you know. Cos you'd been quite ill, hadn't you, quite up and
down, depressed and that. So everyone was saying to me,
explaining that you'd, you know. But I absolutely knew you
hadn't. I knew I just had to... I mean that's when I started
really. Thinking outside the box.

Thought if you hadn't gone along the beach, which you hadn't
cos, no footprints, and you hadn't gone, you know. I mean you
definitely hadn't gone in the sea. So, logically, you must have
gone: up. And you must have gone up fast enough to leave your
sandals behind, which happened once on a ride at Alton Towers
but it has to be flipping fast. Flipping, alien fast. Like in a beam
sort of thing.

So then I knew.

After that it was just a case of reading up on astrophysics,
antimatter, learning the space languages, and they're all on the
internet. Found this theory about how ninety-seven per cent of the
universe is actually made up of loneliness – that's on the internet
too. Just a case of reading all that, building some basic tracking
devices, waiting for the signals to come together. Which is today.

And I explain all this to Carl and he just. He doesn't say
anything but sort of bites his lip like he's really anxious.
Probably about the spacewang but I just think: 'Man up, Carl.'
Isn't time for any of that, it's twenty to seven so we just check
the coast's clear, set off.

It's a bit cold but. Carl gives me his coat.

Phase three: the welcome back

Sea's calm tonight. Carl isn't.

He keeps going on about plan Bs. I'm like 'shut up I don't need a
Plan B' but he doesn't stop, he's all: 'Sometimes, Nora, when you
really want something to happen, it is also nice to have a Plan B.'
I just roll my eyes like 'whatever' but he's not giving up. 'Even if
there's just a tiny risk something might not work out'…

NORA *takes out the shoebox, turns on the flashing lights, puts
on the colander and takes a few readings.*

…'even if it's definitely the thing you most want to happen in
the world, sometimes it's good to have a think what you might
do if it turned out a bit. If it turned out different.'

I give him a furious look. He doesn't get it though.

NORA *kneels down, opens the shoebox, takes out a pair of
sandals and places them neatly on the floor.*

'Like, imagine she didn't come tonight. Nora.'

'She's coming tonight.'

'Just in case though. What would you do instead?'

A moment.

'What would be the best thing you'd do instead?'

Silence.

'What if we had fish and chips? Nora? Golden Haddock. And
then you, you can show me your ceiling. With the stars and
everything. We could have a dance. That song you like, that's
like: 'Don't stop believing'… That sound alright? Like an
alright Plan B? If we just…'

But I'm not listening cos. Six fifty-nine p.m.

NORA *gets out some sparklers.*

Carl's a bit surprised at the sparklers. But it's just cos I thought,
if I'd travelled billions of light years through different
dimensions and galaxies and that, and ninety-seven per cent of
what I'd seen was loneliness, and I was feeling sort of, proper
homesick, and knackered and grumpy and bored, I thought: what

would be the thing I'd most like to see when I got to earth? And it just came to me really suddenly: Dolly Parton. But then she's quite hard to, you know. So this was the next best thing.

Give one to Carl an' all.

NORA *lights her sparkler. Checks her watch.*

Fifteen seconds.

She stands with it above her head. Looks up.

You better come now, Mum. I flipping hope you come.

Fade.

A Nick Hern Book

The Kitchen Sink first published in Great Britain as a paperback original in 2011 by Nick Hern Books Limited, 14 Larden Road, London W3 7ST in association with the Bush Theatre, London

Reprinted 2012

The Kitchen Sink copyright © 2011 Tom Wells
Spacewang copyright © 2011 Tom Wells

Cover image by Mat Dolphin/photo by Fabio De Paola
Cover designed by Ned Hoste, 2H

Typeset by Nick Hern Books, London
Printed in the UK by Mimeo Ltd, Huntingdon, Cambridgeshire PE29 6XX

A CIP catalogue record for this book is available from the British Library

ISBN   978 1 84842 222 3

Woodland
CARBON
www.woodlandcarbon.co.uk
NICK HERN BOOKS
Printed on Carbon Captured paper